Praise for BIG ROCKS

From London, England

"Okay now, be honest. Have you ever got up on a morning, looked in the mirror, and muttered, "Geez ... I'm not sure who's more frightened ... me or the mirror"? Well, I know it's true that my outer appearance really is a true reflection of my inner self, and it can be scary sometimes! Thankfully, after reading this book, my mirror smiles back at me more every day ... bet yours will, too."

• Christine Lightfoot
Managing Director, Idea Law

From Washington, DC

"Gary Russell's book is essential reading for all in need of prioritizing daily demands on their time. The book provides a compass, as well as practical tips and basic principles, for capitalizing on available time and changing one's life for the better."

• Attorney James L. Bikoff
Partner, Silverberg, Goldman & Bikoff

From South Africa

"Just what we all need, another book telling us how to balance our busy lives ... except this book has the X factor. It doesn't just motivate and inspire; the examples in the book show you how to realistically balance your every day. It's not just about balance, though; it's about fulfillment and enrichment of life."

• Rachael Gasco
Member Services Coordinator, Cannons

From Abingdon, England

"I first discovered the Big Rocks workshop at a time in my life when I was treading water but struggling to keep my head above it! Discovering simple tools to balance my priorities gave me one of my most prized life lessons. It made me realize that I have the choice to either fall off the precipice or make a planned ascent into the rest of my life. Realizing that I can make the choices gives me confidence for the future, for my son, and for myself; wherever I take my life. Thank you, Gary."

• Sarah Pearce
Marketing and Communications Support Manager, CLS

BIG ROCKS

BALANCING LIFE & WORK

DR. GARY F. RUSSELL

A LifeStyle Press
Publication

For information address LifeStyle Press Publications, 100 South Street, Suite 202, Sausalito, CA 94965.

Anyone interested in using this book for educational purposes should visit www.focuslifestyle.org for information on quantity discounts.

Any similarity between the fictional figures or persons or places portrayed in this manuscript and real persons or characters or places is strictly coincidental.

FIRST EDITION

Designed by Stephanie Huntwork

Library of Congress Cataloging-in-Publication Data

Russell, Dr. Gary F. (Gary Ford), 1944 –
    Big Rocks: Balancing Life & Work / Dr. Gary F. Russell
cm.
Includes bibliographical references and index
ISBN 0-9701331-1-1

1. Balancing Work & Life   2. Alignment   3. Time Management
4. Strategic Planning   5. Harmony   6. Family Values

There is usually one beacon of light that gives us guidance, inspiration, and direction. Combine that with unconditional caring and love, and you gain purpose and meaning, which make a life that is balanced and fulfilled.

This book is dedicated to my BIG ROCK, my wife, Nanci, for without her and the inspiration she provides, this story of balancing life and work would not exist.

I love you, woman.

—B. D.

CONTENTS

ACKNOWLEDGMENTS

First and foremost I would like to thank my families—both my immediate family and my extended work family.

To my wife, Nanci, for her daily inspiration in my life and for always believing I would get this book written eventually. To my children, Brett, Carrie, Chris, and Beckie, for their support and valuable input. Additionally, to my son Chris, who like my other children amazes me every day—but you, son, have a gift: to write and inspire. Thank you for sharing your gift and adding your own writing touch to this book.

To my work family at MLS Camps and The Focus Group: Ian Tonks, Paul Read, Roy Collins, Neil Castle, Dave Newbury, Ginger Asher, Billie Shea, Helen Castle, Jacqie Grillo, Susan Dombrowski, Michelle Riley, Krista May, Katie Rowson, Deven Apajee, Adam Gee, Dave Asprey, Dave Baker, Dave Jervis, Gary Overton, Andy Farley, James Hippett, Brian Boatman, Carl Blakey, Alec Cruickshank, Neil Diaz, Barry Mantle, Adrian Moses, Tom Allgier, Jamie Martin, Joe Dixon, Jonny Mould, Justin Hale, Lee Eastbourne, Mark Hodson, Matt Brown, Mike Elias, Olly Bayliss, Paul Murphy, Richard Kirk, Richard Kopplin, Scott Benbow, Scott Buss, Scott Reynolds, Sean Coffey, and Spencer Harris. Thanks for believing in my continuous training efforts and putting my philosophies into action and driving business success. Additionally, to Neil, Helen, Ian, and Ginger—thanks for reviewing the first draft with such enthusiasm.

To Billie Shea, who has worked with me for many years and had the patience and gift of translating all my ideas so that others would gain. Without you, the rest of the world wouldn't have had the opportunity to grow beyond its vision of capability.

To my team of first-draft reviewers, who took the time to give me positive feedback and valuable constructive criticism. Your efforts made this final product so much better. Thank you, Joan Shea, Louise Dagger, Rachel Gasco, Paul Johnson, Chris Lightfoot, Christine Lightfoot, Sarah Pearce, Grace Sutherland, Tom Wenrich, and Betty-Sue Schaughency.

I would also like to recognize the researchers who, in addition to my own research, have published materials that support the principles behind the BIG ROCKS strategy. I have made a special effort to highlight such research notes throughout this text for any reader who is interested in gaining a deeper knowledge of a specific topic not addressed in this work. I would like to extend a special thanks to my partners and friends at the Gallup Organization—specifically Tom Rath, Pio Juszkiewicz, and Larry Emond—for providing me with research, guidance, and tips on best practices for editing and publishing this work.

A special thank-you to Allison Bacewicz for jumping in headfirst and organizing all of the research referenced in this book.

Thank you to all of the beautiful teachers in northeast Ohio who taught me about my own work and helped me to clarify what is important for children and their families.

Finally, I would like to thank anyone who has ever attended a BIG ROCKS workshop. The positive feedback that I continuously gain from you provided the inspiration to write this book so that a wider audience could learn about the BIG ROCKS strategy.

Introduction

Twenty-three years ago my wife and I had a conversation that forever changed the course of my life. She said, "If we're going to live like this, then there's no reason to be married anymore." That was my wake-up call and one of the most pivotal moments of my life. Back then I was an entrepreneur trying to make a success of my first business. To me, success meant working seven days a week, seventeen hours a day. I put so much time and energy into my work that I had nothing left for anyone or anything else. Essentially, my wife was a married woman living a single life. If I wanted to save our relationship, I had to make some changes. It was an easy choice because of course I wanted my marriage to work—doesn't everyone?

It was at that moment that I recognized how out of balance my life had become. Although I was putting all of my effort into my work for the right reasons, I was getting the wrong results. I was frightened because I knew I had to change my behavior to improve my marriage, but I had no idea where to begin. So, with a fair amount of trial and error, I began my own personal journey toward putting more balance into my life. Since that time, I've made it a priority to take a leadership role in helping others to do the same.

I believe very strongly that most people's lives are out of balance. The causes vary widely depending on the individual, but internal and external forces contribute to the imbalance most of us feel in our lives. My belief has grown from my years serving as a chief executive officer running my own corporation. During this time, I have conducted and studied research, provided training, and taught workshops aiming to elevate the quality of life for countless people throughout the United States and Europe. My formal and anecdotal research coupled with my passion to stay current with the issues and events that define our society is the fuel that drove me to write this book.

One workshop that I have been conducting for years has consistently delivered positive results. It is called BIG ROCKS, and this book grew out of that concept. The BIG ROCKS strategy focuses on the issue of balance because the struggle to "fit it all in" surfaces time and again in our lives.

As a society, we are under a tremendous amount of stress, causing us to feel rushed and agitated. We are lost in our hurried lives and often feel as though our voices are not being heard. We are challenged to find the time to enjoy our lives outside work. These sentiments are reflected in countless personal stories that I have listened to, and while the faces telling the stories change, the central "pain point" remains the same.

The inspiration for this book has come from my family and friends as well as my colleagues and countless workshop participants. I am grateful for their support and hope I have done their messages justice. The premise grew from experiential data gathered from interactions with thousands of workshop participants who have adopted the Focus Lifestyle™ and actively follow the BIG ROCKS strategy. This book, although written as a parable to reach out to the broadest possible audience, is grounded in decades of research. Many of the facts and opinions contained herein were developed from a combination of organizational research, leading business research, and my own behavioral psychology research. The genre I chose for this business-oriented book is a parable. I want you, the reader, to put your feet in the shoes of the main character and experience a BIG ROCKS workshop. When you meet Jack Bedford, I think you will find a little of yourself in him. You may even find a little of yourself in his wife, Lisa, or other characters you meet along the way.

This book is more than just a parable because it is interactive. As Jack Bedford goes through the workshop, he completes a series of activities and worksheets. You may complete your own activities and worksheets along with Jack. My goal is for you to be not only a reader of the story but a participant in it. I believe this book is timely, and I hope the style in which it is written will resonate with you. I know I can see things more clearly when I can live them through someone else's experience.

Times have changed, and so has the world we live in. We all know change is inevitable, yet some of us still have a hard time adapting while trying to balance our lives. This book provides a solution to the chronic challenge of achieving and maintaining balance in your life. Balance centers on our ability to effectively filter all of the choices available to us into a personal success formula that allows us to be actively engaged in our daily lives and derive meaning and personal fulfillment from our achievements.

We race to keep pace in the uncharted territory created by rapid societal changes, and as a result we are ill prepared to sort out and prioritize our lives. This book is a tool to teach us how to boil our lives down to the fundamentals and fit in all of the *right* things. It works to solve what I believe is the number-one social challenge of this century: balance.

—Gary F. Russell

ONE

Looking Back

t was my turn. I was ten years old and the seventeenth grandchild of thirty-two. Each of us got to choose one week each year to spend with Grandma at her home in Monaca (MonACKa), Pennsylvania. I remember looking forward to my week with such anticipation that it felt as if it would take days to get there rather than the few minutes it took to travel from my home in nearby Beaver Falls.

I didn't think much about what it actually meant at the time because I was too young to understand the deeper meaning of family ties and building relationships. But to this day I can still recapture that feeling of excitement and pure joy that came over me each time it was my turn with Grandma. We took pleasure in the simple joy of sharing our time together, and we were a top priority for one another during that entire week each year.

Now, as an adult in my midthirties, I yearned to have those very basic needs met as fully as I did then. I longed for the simple enjoyment of another person's company and the feeling of belonging and contentment that comes along with it. It seemed that those feelings that had so easily brought me peace and self-worth back then were now just a distant memory in my life. At the ripe old age of thirty-six, I found myself looking back on my childhood with greater frequency, remembering that time with a much deeper understanding of the lessons I had been taught through the experiences of my youth.

There was a picture on my desk of Grandma and me when I was a little boy of ten. It was taken right before summer began, and Grandma, who apparently thought hair served no purpose during hot weather, had recently shaved my light-blond hair within an inch of its life. If you looked closely, you could even see the two or three spots where the razor had nicked off enough to show smooth white scalp that invariably became sunburned within days. Whereas my eleven-year old son today wouldn't be caught dead with this butchered haircut, back then it simply made me look like I was part of a club, since the rest of the boys in the neighborhood sported the same look. The photo showed Grandma sitting with me on the weathered front porch of her modest Monaca home that always looked in dire need of a paint job but had the most comfortable old wicker chairs I'd ever sat on. She wore what I used to refer to as her "Grandma uniform"—her usual multicolored flowered housecoat and a crisp white apron. She had just finished making me fresh oatmeal cookies, and I had the smile, and crumbs, on my face to prove it.

This cherished photo sat right next to a photo of me with my family taken just a year ago. My wife, Lisa, my son, Jake, and my nine-year-old daughter, Beckie, were smiling at the camera with their faces alight with all the joy they could muster for the hurry-up-and-smile-for-only-$25-in-five-minutes photo shoot. Me? I looked like I was already halfway out of my chair, as if it were on fire. Come to think of it, I remembered having to hurry back home that Sunday to catch up on some reports so I'd be prepared for an important meeting at work on Monday. Still, just seeing all of us together in one place, even for a few moments, made this photo special to me.

My gaze often jumped between the two pictures at various times throughout the day. As it did, I'd find myself thinking about my deep-rooted need to bring those feelings of belonging and contentment back to the forefront of my life with the people who were most important to me. The subtle childhood lessons I learned from my grandma and other family members about love, commitment, and loyalty laid a foundation of values that created a legacy of love I continued to build upon throughout my life. Yet, amidst the hectic and rushed hours of my life, I felt as if I had somehow taken a detour that pulled me away from those simple pleasures. I guess that was why I frequently found myself looking for ways to get back on that road that began in Monaca.

The times I spent with Grandma were some of the best in my life. Located among the rolling hills and smokestacks that were typical of western Pennsylvania in the 1970s, Monaca was a very small town, but its few blocks were filled with the continuous movement of life. Grandma used to say, "If you blink twice while driving through Monaca, you wouldn't even realize we were on the map!" To my young eyes, however, this bustling, tight-knit little town was the equivalent of New York City.

Downtown, the main streets were lined with all the shops necessary to support the town. There was the corner grocer, several small coffee shops, the newspaper stand, pharmacy, billiard hall, several clothing shops, lots of pizza houses, and the barbershop. Of course, back then there was also the staple of every small town—an ice-cream parlor—owned by a man everyone called "Pop." Pop had owned that ice-cream parlor for years, and since he was 168 years old, according to my cousin Bobby, I guess the store was really old, too! When I came to get ice cream, I could always count on Pop pulling the red baseball cap Grandma called part of my "grandson uniform" over my eyes with a gleeful tug. I was impressed that he always remembered my name even though he saw me only a few times during my yearly visit. I'm convinced Grandma gave him a heads-up that I was coming, but back then I used to think he looked forward to seeing his favorite customer each year as much as I did to coming in for my favorite ice-cream cone. Pop used to holler over to Grandma and me as we sat enjoying our ice-cream cones on the paint-chipped green bench outside the front of the store: "You can't buy anything close to my ice cream from Old Mr. Adams, can ya?" Mr. Adams owned the corner grocery store across the street, and he and Pop had a friendly rivalry. Grandma reassured me that they genuinely liked and respected one another and enjoyed their friendly competition. That was just how it was in Monaca … everyone knew each other's lives in detail, and while that kind of closeness sometimes spurred small spats between folks, there was always a bond of loyalty as strong as the iron and steel that was mined in that small town.

Because Monaca was an industrial mining town, Grandma would wake me early each morning and say, "Come on, Jack, you need to get a move on so we can finish our errands before the factory workers break for lunch!" Grandma liked to take her time in town so she could be leisurely in her conversations with her friends and stay on top of all the town news, such as who was getting married or having a baby. She used to tell me with a conspiratorial whisper that it was also a great opportunity to show me off to her friends.

Grandma and I would take walks into town each day, and I remembered how important I felt because Grandma seemed to know everyone. She would center attention on me by introducing me with a happy smile, talking excitedly of our time together, and then exchanging pleasantries with the town folks. "You remember my grandson Jack," she would say. "He's going to make us all proud and play baseball for the Phillies one day! Maybe he'll be the next Mike Schmidt—you should see him throw. He's got quite an arm!"

Grandma made me feel as though I were her only grandchild, not one of thirty-two. What strikes me most today as I look back is how happy people were as they went about their daily work. Compared to today's standards, they didn't have much in terms of material possessions, but it didn't seem to matter to them. They understood the meaning of their work and how it fit into the bigger picture of enriching their lives. Back then, the town's people always took the time to say hello, listening with genuine interest to what was going on in Grandma's life, and mine. They always welcomed me without hesitation because of the common tie we shared—the woman I called "Grandma." I always felt included, felt that I belonged.

Grandma's friends were typical residents of Monaca. They were working or lower middle class, and their husbands, fathers, uncles, and brothers were mostly blue-collar workers engaged in the iron and steel industries. They never thought of their jobs as careers, but they were, nonetheless, built as careers are today—methodically over a lifetime. Trade work was carried through from generation to generation, and loyalty and dedication to work were traits that were admired and respected in Monaca.

Looking back today, I see that those traits were present not only in people's work lives but in their family and social lives as well. Family and social ties were top priorities. This was especially noticeable in the summertime, when I would visit, when there were always local events that took place in the town square. I remember concerts, local art displays, antique sales, and fairs that would be teeming with families from the entire town. Meaning was found in the simple, day-to-day activities of life that were a staple of the community.

During my week with Grandma, she and I would spend day and night together talking, laughing, and playing silly made-up games. I'd jump on the couch in front of the picture window and yell, "Let's play taxicabs!"

Grandma would carefully move all of the family pictures over to the side, and we would play. She and I would sit in front of the one picture window that adorned the front of her tiny home and count the taxicabs as they went by. I was always in awe because Grandma knew every one of the taxicab drivers and threw each one a wave as they passed by. I was too young to understand that the taxicab company owned only five taxicabs and employed an equal number of drivers who made many trips in and out of town in a single day. I was also too young to realize that those taxicabs had to come down our one-way street because it was the only road leading out of town. It seemed that there were a hundred different taxicabs because Grandma and I were counting the same ones over and over again during the game. Once we played so long that I actually counted sixty-three taxicabs. That was a big day.

How I yearned to relive those simple moments. My own two young children would have looked at me as if I had just landed from Mars if I had suggested an activity that did not include TV, the Internet, XBox, or Play-Station.

When we weren't busy counting taxicabs or playing games at home, Grandma would take me out to the baseball games played by the older boys in town. We'd head straight behind the left-field fence because that was where Grandma said we would collect the greatest number of foul balls … and she was right. We would find them, usually in pretty poor condition, well worn and tattered. "Don't worry about what they look like," Grandma would say as she swatted her hand through the air. "I've got a trick that will make any baseball you find look as good as new!"

And she did. Grandma would help me take off all the old covers and then give me what I considered to be my special treat of Johnson and Johnson white adhesive tape. "Wow, am I lucky!" I would think. At the time, almost everyone knew that the tape was used for first-aid purposes, but it would be years before I'd come to realize this. Grandma and I would wrap those tattered baseballs with the tape until they looked and felt like new again. Once we had a good supply of our version of new baseballs, Grandma would say, "Go on out and play, Jack. The neighborhood kids will be glad to have a baseball player as good as you on their team."

Then Grandma would watch from her front yard as I went out to play with the neighborhood kids. The fact that I had what appeared to be very white, new baseballs boosted my popularity. The kids would invite me to play ball with them, often fighting over whose team I'd play for, and Grandma would cheer us on. I felt special and important. And boy, did time fly. I never worried about checking the time or that I had to hurry up and finish to be somewhere else. The baseballs were my contribution, and, believe me, they were appreciated because there wasn't a single one of us who could afford to buy new ones. Looking back now, I understand that the baseballs were the basic link that I used to make connections and build relationships with the neighborhood kids.

Although our family was very poor, we were rich in values, and our family and community ties were unbreakable. There was always a sense of belonging and support. When all thirty-two grandchildren and our respective families gathered for holidays and special events, the noise was deafening—the banging of dishes and doors, the constant buzz of conversations punctuated with bellows of laughter, and the nonstop running of what appeared to be both small and large herds of kids.

Certainly there were times when family members disagreed or fought, but the good times, our shared history, and the strength of our family ties always won out over the disagreements. There was a bond that went deeper than even blood, a connectedness we subconsciously chose to nurture because it fulfilled a need in each of us. Looking more closely at our upbringing, I can easily see how those ties remain strong to this day.

Now, sitting in my office looking back, I could still feel the warmth, the excitement, and the joy that I had felt then. I couldn't prevent my lips from curling into a smile every time I recalled the memories from that period of my life. It was always enjoyable to retell the tales of my childhood with my family members on the too rare occasions when we gathered together now. I now understood that it wasn't the ice-cream cones or the baseballs that made me so wistful for my past. It wasn't the food, or even Monaca itself. The wonderful quality of these memories was really all about how I *felt* during the time Grandma spent with me, and the effort my family made to spend special occasions together, to celebrate life and one another. It was about how we all felt being together and the feeling of belonging to, and being part of, something bigger. It was the connections that were nurtured within my family and within our community. It was about building relationships. We never talked in detail about how much we valued our relationships, and we never uttered the word "quality"—but that was just what it was.

TWO

Back to Reality

Earth to Jack!" shouted my boss, startling me. I looked up to meet his wide-eyed expression. "I need your latest report so I can use it to discuss the numbers in today's executive meeting. Have you printed it out yet?"

I shook myself from my peaceful childhood daydream and could feel my anxiety level rising, not because I hadn't done my work but because of his "bull in a china shop" approach. "Yes," I replied. "I put it on your desk an hour ago."

"Well, I didn't see it and I don't have time to run back upstairs to my office to get it, so could you just print me another copy so I can get into the meeting?"

I looked down to see my own copy sitting on top of my monthly reports. "Here," I said, "take mine. I'll print another one for myself." With that he was gone.

I jumped up, pulled the corner of the blind over slightly, and peered out my office window to see the bank clock across the street. It was 4 P.M. on a Tuesday, and I was sitting in the closed, very ordinary quarters of my office at Rutter Financial Group, Inc. I was busy planning an early, inconspicuous escape as I stared blankly at the new business cards that had been dumped on my desk that morning. They read, "Jack Bedford, Senior Bustomer Service Specialist." "Great," I thought. "There's a typo on my new cards." Oh well, the business cards were a waste of company money since I wouldn't be serving the "bustomers" at Rutter much longer, anyway.

"Hey, Jack," Bob, our company's accountant, shouted over, "is it true that you're leaving us in a few weeks?" He made his way to my desk to learn more, or perhaps to lay claim to any office supplies that might remain after I left.

"Yes, Bob," I replied, unconsciously reaching to hold on to my stapler. "I've found a great job with another firm."

"What are you going to be doing?"

"I'll still be working in the financial industry in a similar position to the one I have here. I just believe there is more room for growth in the new company. The company culture also seems like a great fit for my personality. I'm going to have more autonomy than I do here. I'm looking forward to the change."

"Oh, good for you," said Bob, not even trying to hide his apathy.

I forced a polite laugh and continued, "Well, most days I feel like the kid who is 'officially' part of the team but always sits on the bench and watches the game unfold."

"Just can't find a way to get yourself into the huddle, is that it?" said Bob as he tried to stifle a yawn. "I feel like that a lot, too. I think they hide the motivation around here somewhere. I don't know. I haven't found it yet. Maybe it's just doled out to the new hires and there's a short supply for us veterans. It's just hard to stay motivated for the high number of hours we all put in every week."

"I totally agree. That's also a great thing about my new job," I continued. "According to the three executives I spoke with, I won't have to work any more of these crazy hours. Best of all, there is a high priority placed on family and outside interests. One of the executives has a son only a few years older than Jake, and he says he never misses one of his son's baseball games. He joked around that the work would still be there when he returned. I liked his attitude because I feel like I never have enough time to spend with my family. I had the impression that this guy understands the importance of family and outside interests, and he backs up his beliefs with actions in the way he runs his department."

"Yeah, good luck with that," said Bob as he walked away, sipping his coffee.

"Thanks, Bob," I said as I locked my office supplies in my desk. I shook my head. Bob was brilliant, and he used to be upbeat when I first knew him. Yet the company didn't utilize his talents. Now Bob had succumbed to the monotony of doing what he was told. He had officially become a resentful paycheck collector.

Despite this, sadly, my conversation with Bob was the best one I'd had all day, and it was already 4:15. I needed to get out of the office unnoticed today. Jake's soccer game was at 5 o'clock, and I wanted to be there. His team was undefeated so far this season, 3 and 0. He was playing goalie today, and he really wanted me to see how much better he'd gotten. I knew it meant the world to him when I showed up, even if I was usually late. It felt like my inconspicuous escapes from the office were always blocked or diverted, but today I was going, even if I had to hide in the mail cart to get out. I had to make this game. Quickly I gathered my belongings, sidled along the wall, peeked around the corner, and began my furtive escape.

The challenge at Rutter was that the executives conveyed an unspoken policy of the necessity to work long hours, even if just for show, and that policy was always strongly evident at review and promotion time. Since I was leaving the company, I shouldn't really have cared what they would say about my early exit today, but I wanted my last days to go as smoothly as possible. I didn't want to make any waves in case I needed a future reference.

I'd been conditioned all along to fall in line with Rutter's corporate culture, even though I hated it. It didn't fit my lifestyle, which made me feel resentful toward my work and my employer, even though it was a decent job in other respects. But because it consumed so much of my time and the office atmosphere was so tense, I found that it had a negative impact on other important areas of my life. Between the long hours and my generally cranky disposition at the end of most days, my personal and social lives suffered. Even when I was away from work, I wasn't really away. I was always available via a cell phone, and I often lugged my laptop home in order to keep my head above water in regard to my workload. I always felt stressed.

I did my job the way the executives saw fit, yet my ideas for process improvements or for providing new and valuable services to our customers went unrecognized. I can't tell you how many times I'd heard, "Interesting idea, Jack. We'll take that into consideration." Yet somehow the ideas got lost, and things plodded along the same as always.

At Rutter it seemed that talking about making changes was as far as anything went. The few times anyone attempted to implement a specific change, it was always short-lived. Team spirit seemed to die on the vine and was difficult to cultivate in the top-heavy management structure. There were some hard-and-fast lines in the rankings of employees according to position that couldn't be ignored. Any movement toward change or improvement ultimately went back to everything being done the way it had been done before. I ended up thinking, "Why bother?"

Before my daring escape from the office, I took a little detour and checked in with my coworker Susan. I had to drop off some files for customers I was in the process of handing over to her. Susan was one of the people at Rutter whom I could have a decent conversation with. We shared a lot of the same pains. She was always riddled with guilt about not spending enough time with her teenaged daughter.

Susan was immersed in her work, so I quietly placed the files on the table opposite her desk. "Thanks, Jack," Susan said sarcastically without even looking in my direction. "I'll be sure to stop at Wal-Mart on my way home tonight to buy a sleeping bag."

"What? Why? Are you going camping this weekend?" I asked, not really understanding what she was talking about.

"No, I'm not going camping," she said as she swiveled in her chair to face me. "You know outdoor bathroom facilities and no electricity aren't my style! I just meant that once you leave Rutter I'll have to start spending nights here just to get all my work done. Haven't you heard? They're not planning to replace you right away. They're going to divide your customers up among the rest of us and 'see how it goes.' You should stick around a few more weeks just to watch *that* circus!"

My shoulders sank and my eyes widened. "I had no idea," I said clumsily. I could feel her anxiety. "Umm, did you want me to put these files somewhere else? I don't mean to be rude, but I need to get to Jake's game by 5 P.M."

"Actually, if you could just put them on Janette's desk, that will give me room to organize my own files before I integrate yours. Janette's not going to be back anytime soon," Susan said through gritted teeth. "She's still out on workman's compensation. It's been three months now, and apparently her chronic carpal-tunnel syndrome is still active. The latest update is that she won't be back for another three weeks to a month, which is fine. It's actually kind of nice not to have to listen to the constant droning of her negativity. She always said that Rutter would be sorry because she was going to make them pay. You've got to hand it to her—she's true to her word!" Susan gave me a forced smile to break the tension.

"That's interesting. I just saw Janette several weeks ago. She was riding her bike just outside town, and if you can believe it," I said in a whisper, "she was actually smiling. Maybe bike rides are part of the therapy." We shared a chuckle and a simultaneous eye-roll.

"Suze, I'll just set the files over here on Janette's desk. I'll see you tomorrow … and by the way, I think you should check out Target instead. They were having a sale on sleeping bags."

"Thanks," Susan groaned as she crumpled up a piece of paper and threw it at me. "You're the lucky one, you know. You've managed to get out!" She chuckled. "I'm happy for you, Jack. You'd just better call me if it ends up being a great place to work and another opening for an equities manager comes up."

"You know I will," I said. "I feel bad leaving you in this mess. It's so typical, isn't it, Suze? No one looks out for each other here. It's so chaotic, and while you're working your tail off, people like Janette are out riding their bikes and collecting checks. I always feel as if we're all being set up to fail— that nothing is ever good enough. Why does there have to be such a great divide between the executives and the rest of us? They want us to keep bringing in business, but they forget to give us enough support. Minor oversight. When was the last time you were offered any help—or better yet, skills training?"[1]

"I can't remember," said Susan. "I do vaguely remember a time-management seminar several years back, but I can't say anything changed. But it was certainly worth the price of admission just to spend a day away from the office! You're right, though, there are very few avenues for us to improve our skills. And even if there were, I honestly don't know where I'd find the time to take advantage of them."

"I hear you. All right, I've got to go or I'll be late for Jake's game."

With that parting comment, I headed for the door. I chuckled to myself as I walked briskly through the office. All I could think as I scanned the office was that we at Rutter were a motley crew. The disgruntled administrative staff was a fine example. The running joke around the office was that our clocks would never be stolen because the administrative staff was too busy watching them. I noticed Judy reading the latest issue of *Cosmopolitan,* hidden underneath some company report.

I turned the corner, and there sat Tom logged on to ESPN.com, reading about the Red Sox and their World Series win. He had a look of despair on his face because he was a Yankees fan. I would almost have felt slightly sorry for him if I hadn't been a huge Red Sox fan (much to the chagrin of my grandmother) burdened with uncontrollable joy about Boston's historic win. What can I say, Yankees fans were just not equipped to handle this kind of trauma—losing the playoffs when they were up by three games in the series. My people were better equipped to handle that sort of thing. We had more experience with it. However, that experience had certainly made victory that much sweeter! "How do you like us now, New York?" I whispered to myself as I reached for the door. Carly was talking on the telephone to her boyfriend; she paused until the door slowly closed behind me, but I knew the drill. I didn't see Joe, but he was usually anywhere but at his desk. I think most of his day was one big coffee break.

I'd actually had days when you might have thought I'd asked one of the administrative assistants to personally grow wings to fly a package to a customer when I had simply wanted a Federal Express pickup to be scheduled. This frustration contributed to my own long hours and discontent.

I'd made it out the door, and I sprinted to my car. Once I was on the road, I called my wife to let her know I was on my way.

"Hey, Lisa, it's me. Have you left work yet?"

"Yes, I'm at the field right now. Where are you?"

"I'm just leaving work now."

"Oh, good," she said, and I could hear the relief in her voice. "Jake's really looking forward to your being here, and Beckie made you a present today in school." I could hear Beckie talking in the background. In her excitement she spilled the beans and told me she'd made me a necklace of shells. "Obviously she can't wait to give it to you! Also … hold on just a minute." I could hear Lisa talking with someone in the background. She came back on the line and told me that Dave Klein, the assistant coach for Jake's team, wanted to speak with me. She handed the phone over to Dave.

"Hi, Dave," I said.

"Jack, could you help me out coaching the team today?" asked Dave. "Josh had to leave unexpectedly due to a family matter."

"Sure," I said. "I'm still in my work clothes, but I'll be on the sidelines with you in about ten minutes."

Lisa came back on the line. "Where are you now?"

"On Route 84, about ten minutes away. I may be a few minutes late, but tell Jake I'm on my way, and tell Beckie I can't wait to see the necklace!"

"You can wear it while you coach," joked Lisa. "Maybe it will bring Jake's team more luck." I could hear Beckie agreeing in the background. "How was your day today, Jack?"

"Urrggghh. More of the same."

"Well, the good news is you only have seven more work days at Rutter, and then you won't have to run around like a crazy person anymore! Oh ... hang on again, Jack."

I was concentrating on the road and had missed Lisa's last comment. "I love you," I said.

"I love you, too," replied Dave Klein's gruff voice. "Don't worry, Jack, I won't tell your wife! But seeing as you love me, could you run into the locker room before you come over to the field and grab the water jug for the kids?"

I laughed and agreed to grab the water. "I'll see you soon," I said as I sped up just a little to get to the game.

The example that had been set for me, growing up in a small western Pennsylvania town, had made me think that my own daily life as an adult would be simple. The reality was that it wasn't simple at all, and no one had ever really taken the time to teach me that. Somehow I assumed that managing my life in adulthood would come naturally. It didn't. I had found myself reflecting on my childhood with greater frequency lately—most notably on the joy that was always present and those memorable childhood experiences with family and friends. What I hadn't had the capacity to understand as a child was suddenly becoming clearer to me.

I knew it was natural for everyone to look ahead and work to improve their future. However, at the present time, I felt a strong need to change my life—a major overhaul. I wondered if this was my midlife crisis. If it was, there was a bright side—I'd always told my wife I'd buy a new Jaguar when my midlife crisis hit.

I pulled into the parking lot at the school for Jake's game. As I grabbed the jug of water from the locker room and made my way out to the field, I realized that by reflecting on the past I was beginning to gain perspective on what was missing from my life.

Interestingly enough, it was a chance meeting with a stranger at Jake's game, and accepting his advice from the sidelines, that ultimately changed my life.

THREE

Advice from the Sidelines

I attempted to jog over to the team's bench on the sidelines, but it was too difficult to move quickly carrying the water. The twenty-five pounds I'd gained over the past few years weren't helping my cause. I was out of breath by the time I reached the bench and had just missed seeing Jake's team score its first goal. I looked out on the field to find Jake and saw that he was busy high-fiving his best friend, Kevin Morin. Those two had been friends since before they could walk. Kevin lived just three houses down from us.

As I watched Jake and Kevin celebrate their goal, I asked myself why we as adults don't celebrate the little things as Jake and Kevin were doing right now. People and their accomplishments weren't celebrated.[1] I envied how easy it was for Jake and Kevin to maintain their friendship, and I began to wonder, "What happened when we became adults? Why do relationships seem so much more difficult?"

Relationships are fragile. Too often people walk away from them because it's easier than working them out. I glanced over to see Kevin's mom, Melissa, sitting on the bleachers. Kevin's dad had left over three years ago, and Melissa was now a single mom trying to raise two boys on her own. It frightened me that more than half the marriages in this country end in divorce. A simple coin toss could determine whether your marriage would succeed or fail.[2]

"Hi," said a familiar voice from behind me. I turned to say hello to my wife and accept the present from my daughter.

"Will you wear it now, Daddy?" squealed Beckie as she moved closer to try to put the necklace around my neck. I bent down to make it easier for her and stole a kiss. I stood up, and Lisa and I watched a huge grin crawl across Beckie's face as she admired her own work. I gave Lisa a kiss on the cheek.

"We're going to be sitting right behind you with Melissa," said Lisa.

I watched Lisa and Beckie go sit down, and all I could think of was how lucky I was to have my family. Man, I really loved them. If there was any reason why I needed to get my life back on track, it was them.

Jake finally saw me and threw me a wave as both teams got into position to resume the game. The opposing team got the game started again and raced down the field trying to score a goal. We were twenty-five minutes into the first half, and Jake's team was winning 1-0.

A goal attempt was made, and Jake dove to stop it. "Great stop, Jake!" I shouted. As Jake kicked the ball away, my mind trailed back to my own thoughts. I was still nursing pangs of guilt about all the pressure that was going to be put on Susan when I left Rutter. I couldn't believe they weren't going to fill my position right away. I wondered what the executives could possibly be thinking. Suddenly, I realized that a lot of eyes were on me. I had been standing there shaking my head back and forth in disbelief at what I was thinking, and I must have looked a bit kooky! I began to swat my hands frantically around my head so people would think I had simply been trying to avoid the many mosquitoes. I accompanied these actions with an understanding smile to those who made eye contact with me to indicate that I knew they agreed with me about these pesky insects. They continued to stare. That was when I realized they were waiting for me to swap a couple of players. I hurriedly made the replacements, but, even after that embarrassing display of insanity, my mind immediately went right back to my frustration.

I couldn't be the only one on the planet struggling to manage all of the things in my busy life, could I? Why was I spending all of my time thinking about this? I needed to *do* something about it. I certainly understood the concept of achieving balance in my life, and I believed in it. Now I had to act to achieve a balance between my work life and my personal life or I believed these thoughts would monopolize more time than they should. They were already draining the fun out of the few activities in my life that were supposed to be fun.

Jake's team came to the sidelines, interrupting my thoughts and reflections. "Great half," I said to the team as I put my hand on Jake's shoulder and patted it for a job well done. "Great stop!"

"Thanks, Dad ... and thanks for filling in today," Jake said with a big grin. "I wish you could go back to coaching all the time!"

"Me, too," I said as I jumped into laying out the team's strategy for the second half. When the boys got back onto the field, my mind raced unwillingly back to my obsession with trying to figure out what was wrong with the people at Rutter.

Out of the corner of my eye, I noticed that my son had just made a great play on the soccer field, and I cheered loudly and boisterously as any proud parent would: "Yeah, Jake. Great tackle! You go!" Then I realized other parents were looking at me strangely. This was happening too much today. I turned to Kevin Morin's mom and asked, "What?"

She replied, "That's not Jake, Jack. That's Bill Taylor's boy, Jeff."

Oh, jeez, I couldn't even keep my mind in the game enough to recognize my own son! Some dad I was today.

The game resumed, and the runaway train I called my mind took off again. Like me, I thought many people lived their lives from the outside looking in, as a spectator instead of a participant. As I watched my son's soccer game wind down, I realized that I wanted to be a participant in my own life just as my son was being a participant at that very moment. I'd been a spectator far too long. I now recognized that by allowing myself to sit on the sidelines in my own life, I had become unplugged.

Now, that was an epiphany. When you're a spectator, you have no control over the outcome of the game. Okay, maybe you can cheer and shout really loudly to inspire those in the game so that for a fleeting moment you have the illusion of control. But the only way to gain control is to get into the game and play. Everyone needed to participate. Our own lives were no different. If we looked for specific outcomes, we needed to participate in making them happen. Otherwise, as spectators, we could easily assume the role of victim and genuinely believe we were owed. We could even begin to believe that it was someone else's responsibility to fix our discontentment. We could look outside ourselves to resolve our issues and expect great returns on poor investments. Now I was beginning to describe many people I knew.

I stopped myself for a moment to make a conscious effort to watch the game. I found myself sitting back and watching all the kids interact, work together, and celebrate each small victory with high fives, cheers, and words of encouragement. The irony was that it was us—the adults—who had taught those kids to interact that way. Why didn't we do the same? As adults, we had forgotten how to play. If play was like oxygen to children, then I figured it had to be the same for adults because at that point in my life I was gasping for air.

"Coach, don't look so worried. We're winning the game, you know," I heard a man's voice say from behind me. I turned to see a man whose face I recognized because he was at every game. Yet I couldn't remember his name. I knew he had cheered wildly when we had scored our third goal, and I knew his son's name was Chris.

"Huh?" I said, surprised. "Uh, yeah, I was just thinking how great it would be if that kind of teamwork and celebration happened at work."

"It should be that way," the man said.

"Is that your boy?" I asked him.

"Yeah, that's my son, Chris, number 8," the man replied. "Which number is your son? Does he play for the Tornadoes?"

"Yes, he's number 12," I said.

"Oh, Jake Bedford," the man said knowingly. "He's a solid player. You must be proud. Wait a minute. I recognize you. Didn't you help coach the team last season?"

"Yes, I did. I'm Jack, Jack Bedford."

"Tom Baker. Nice to meet you, Jack," he replied as he extended his hand, still maintaining one eye on the field.

"I assisted in coaching Jake's team for the past two seasons. Unfortunately, I couldn't fit it in this season. I really miss it. These days, I'm just thankful when I can make a game on time, or at all for that matter. Josh, the regular coach, had an unexpected family matter to attend to, so I'm filling in."

"Well, at least they still call you to do that," Tom said enthusiastically. "I understand where you're coming from, though, when it comes to being here to support your son. I come to all of Chris's games. I haven't missed one yet. I love coming early to watch them warm up and watch the anticipation build before the start of the game." Tom continued, "It's fun to be part of the celebration afterward if they win, or even part of the 'let's get 'em next time' support if they don't. You and Jake should join us over at Village Pizza after the game."

"You know what? I think I'll take you up on that, Tom." After a short pause, which I used to figure out how to tactfully ask my next question, I said, visibly perplexed, "How are you able to make all of Chris's games at different schools in the middle of the afternoon? Today's game is actually later than normal; I rarely make the 3 o'clock games. I mean, I'm not trying to pry, but are you independently wealthy, Lotto winner, own your own business, unemployed?"

Tom laughed. "Independently wealthy or Lotto winner would be nice," he said. "But no, I have a full-time job. I work for a national sporting-goods distributor called CSAN [pronounced C-san]. We have a really great team of people. Most of us have children of varying ages. We try to arrange our schedules in a way that allows everyone to meet both their personal and professional commitments. All of us staff have very strong relationships that extend even beyond work, and we have systems in place that allow us to cover for one another if we need to be away from the office."

"Are you kidding me? Does your boss know about this strategy, or do you just keep him tied up in an office until he is forced to agree?" I asked.

Tom chuckled and said, "Yes, he knows. In fact, he was the mastermind behind allowing us to structure our own work environment to meet our needs. He was speaking at an executive conference and he had some time to kill, so he attended one of the other management tracks. He told us he was impressed with a presentation called 'BIG ROCKS!' He said he was really blown away by the information and the simplicity of the BIG ROCKS strategy for creating balance in your life. He felt so strongly about it that he sent all of us to the same workshop a few months later. After the workshop we were all very enthusiastic, so we convened and formulated a plan using the BIG ROCKS strategy that has worked famously ever since."

"BIG ROCKS, huh?" I asked with a sideways glance that no doubt made him feel a little silly.

"Jack, I know where you're coming from. I was once there myself." At that point the celebration on the field caused us to turn our attention back to the game. The final minute of the game was winding down, and the boys had managed to hold the other team 3 to 1. They remained undefeated.

After the celebrating calmed down and both teams said "good game" to one another and slapped hands, I followed Tom's suggestion and took Jake and Kevin out for pizza. Lisa and Beckie headed home, and I told Melissa I'd have Kevin home in an hour or so. Many of Jake's teammates came along, too. They were having a blast, and the joy was contagious. It reminded me again that my life just didn't reflect the connectedness I had felt in my childhood. Clearly, being a part of events like this was one of the things I needed to do more to regain that connectedness.

I sat next to Tom as the boys continued to retell the game's greatest moments to one another. Tom and I jumped in and out of their conversation. "Great job on defense during the last ten minutes of the game," Tom said with a smile. "The other team was painfully close to scoring a goal, and you were all able to work together and hold them back!"

"How about Jake's diving midair catch to block the goal at the end of the first half?" exclaimed Kevin. "The crowd went nuts!" In that instant, I knew that these were the moments I didn't want to miss out on. I wanted to make Jake feel just as important and special as Grandma used to make me feel.

Tom and I spent the remainder of our time at the pizza restaurant involved in our kids' conversation. It was a welcome break from my stressful day. We finished our pizza and said our good-byes.

"Tom, great talking with you today," I said as we were leaving. "If you wouldn't mind, I'd like to give you my e-mail address. If you have any materials on BIG ROCKS, I'd be interested in reading them. If for no other reason than that I'm intrigued by the name," I added with a smile as I wrote my personal e-mail address on a card. "In all seriousness, I'd be interested in learning how to create a work environment like the one you described earlier. Maybe BIG ROCKS will be helpful."

"If you're thinking along those lines, you may just find yourself very interested in the BIG ROCKS strategy I'm talking about," said Tom. "I swear it feels like it's changed our entire company's lifestyle. I think I have some of the workshop materials at the office. I also have some materials from my company on how we've implemented the strategy. Although I have to tell you, you really need to check out the workshop yourself. It helps so much when you get to participate in it. I'll forward you the materials and a website link so you can find out if the workshop is being offered in this area anytime soon."

"Thanks. I'd really appreciate that," I said as I handed him my e-mail address. "See you at the next game … if I can make it," I said with a wry smile.

I climbed into the car, and Jake, Kevin, and I began to make our way home. Jake smiled at me and said, "Thanks, Dad!" and then he and Kevin went back to retelling the game's greatest moments yet again. I thought about how good the moment felt.

FOUR

New Job, Old Problems

My final days at Rutter were uneventful. My farewell party was interesting, to say the least. It felt more as if they were paying last respects than wishing me luck. Most of the people who did show up came out of duty rather than a genuine desire to wish me well. A few people were sincere, and several said they wished they were in my shoes. As I got into my car to leave the parking lot at Rutter for the last time, all I felt was relief.

I had the entire following week off before I began my new job, and it was so relaxing. I felt as though a huge weight had been lifted from my shoulders. I spent time catching up with my wife and kids and getting small tasks done around the house. I made it to both of my son's soccer games, watched my daughter's dance class, and took them both out for ice cream a couple of times after school. We had time for board games at night, soccer practices on the lawn with the neighborhood kids, and several family dinners out. I found that my elevated mood was contagious and worked well to alleviate the previous tensions that had existed among all of us. While the kids were at school and my wife was at work, I spent time getting back into a fitness routine and preparing for my new position at Columbia Management Company (CMC) as an equities manager. My journey toward something better was finally happening. I felt good about my new beginning and life all around. I felt a new sense of enthusiasm and hopefulness that I hadn't felt in a long time.

Before I knew it, my week off had flown by and Monday morning had arrived. I was a little anxious, but mostly I was looking forward to getting started and settling into my new position.

I was up early and managed to get in a three-mile run before getting myself ready and seeing Jake and Beckie off to school. "Good luck today," said Lisa as we walked out to our cars together. "Here," she said, handing me a bag. "I made you lunch for your first day."

"Thanks." With a quick kiss, we were both off to work. I arrived just a few minutes before 9 A.M. I was greeted, shown to my new office, and then introduced around. My colleagues were friendly, and several extended offers to help get me settled in and bring me up to speed on company routines and procedures. I met with Human Resources to take care of logistics and was assigned an administrative assistant who helped me get organized. Her name was Kate, and she patiently walked me through the setup of the computer system, my e-mail, and phone procedures. She explained the rules and procedures of corporate communications policies and then began to help me build my schedule with the other equities managers and the executive management team. Kate informed me that companywide meetings would be automatically downloaded to my calendar and that executives might, on occasion, assign meetings for potential new accounts. Also, when any of the equities managers were out sick or on vacation, Kate explained that their work was distributed among the others. "Each of the equities managers has a team backup," she told me. "Your teammate is Rich Riley. Rich is responsible for covering your accounts when you are absent, and vice versa. It will be your job to set up a schedule and meet with Rich regularly so you are both up to speed on each other's accounts."

This sounded great to me, I thought as Kate was talking. I couldn't imagine returning from vacation and not finding a huge stack of work piled up. Kate moved on to explain weekly scheduling and the system that must be used.

"Don't worry," Kate said reassuringly. "You will be given plenty of notice about any appointment that someone else schedules on your behalf. Be sure to include all of your appointments on your schedule, even your personal ones. That way we can avoid scheduling errors." That sounded promising, I thought.

Next I met with Rich Riley and then the entire group of equities managers. At that point, I was assigned a caseload of customer accounts. I was told that over the next thirty days I would be working in partnership with a senior manager to learn the ropes for customer interaction, documentation, and sales enhancements. So far, so good, I thought.

Over the next several weeks, I began to settle in and familiarize myself with the company's routines and procedures. I felt as though I was catching on quickly, and so far I was getting along very well with my coworkers. Rich and I had decided to meet every Monday morning at 9:15 A.M., just before our team meeting, to bring one another up to speed on our workload. So far the meetings had been strictly about work. No one had shared much information about him- or herself or asked me to lunch or anything, but I was new and training me was keeping everyone busy. Besides, no one ever seemed to go out for lunch anyway.

The only downside during the first several weeks was that I had to miss my son's games because it was a learning period. My schedule was fairly rigid while the executives were managing my progress, but I could live with that temporarily because I knew that once I was fully trained, the management of my schedule would be my sole responsibility, as had been discussed in my original interview.

I was still confident that this work environment could actually accommodate my needs. I had some work to do with regard to building stronger relationships with my coworkers; however, my wife had noticed a change in me and commented on my more pleasant disposition.

Five months passed quickly, and some of my old frustrations had crept back into my life. This new job wasn't the lifestyle change I'd thought it would be. Maybe I had just wanted it to be true so badly that I had actually seen things that weren't quite there. Soccer season was long over, and the only game I had been able to make out of the five that remained when I had started this job was Jake's last. He understood because we'd talked about the job being new, and I had promised that it would get better as he transitioned into basketball season. But I was still struggling. Basketball season came and went, and I made only one game. The number of hours I worked per week had increased by about seven or eight, and new account leads kept piling into my schedule. Now I understood why no one here went to lunch. Company executives were pleased with my job performance and trusted that I could handle more work efficiently.

Executives acted as though I should have been flattered by the influx of new accounts due to my success, but their praise didn't seem genuine. They said things such as, "Because you did such a great job with the Johnson account, we're going to give you a new one to take on. You are truly an asset to the equities team, and we need you on this!" At first I was, in fact, flattered, but then I overheard the same executive saying the exact same thing to several others. Now I felt like they just said things to boost our egos before we had a chance to explain that we didn't have the capacity to take on more. One of my coworkers had recently made a comment in frustration when she was handed two more accounts. She had said, "What's it going to take for them to realize that we need a few more equities managers?" Someone else had chimed in that it was going to take another "mass exodus." When I heard those sentiments, I had a sinking feeling in my gut. All I could think was, new job, same old issues.

As defeat started to creep back into my life, I found myself reflecting on what my friend Tom Baker had spoken to me about after Jake's soccer game when I was still working for Rutter. I remembered his BIG ROCKS strategy. Maybe I should get serious about learning more. And maybe, just maybe, I could also interest some of the folks here in the strategy. When I got home, I was going to dig out Tom's e-mail and find out when and where I could learn more. I had to get back to work at achieving my original goal of finding more balance. If things continued at this new company the way they had been, then I was afraid that this move would turn out to have been a huge mistake—yet another tough learning experience along the winding road to finding and maintaining balance.

FIVE

Taking Initiative: Learning About BIG ROCKS

The room at the Marriott Hotel where the BIG ROCKS seminar was taking place was large and open, but somehow the arrangement of furniture made it comfortable and inviting. After I signed in and collected my presentation materials at the entrance, a gentleman greeted me, handed me a rock about the size of my fist, smiled, and introduced himself as Bill. He welcomed me to the seminar and didn't seem insulted when I stared quizzically at his strange "gift." He encouraged me to grab a bite to eat along with some coffee and make myself comfortable. I listened as he welcomed the people behind me in the same warm and genuine manner. I'd never been to a workshop that had a greeter before. Then again, I'd never been handed a rock before either. … This could be interesting.

I made my way over to the semicircle of chair rows, and I was forced to sit up front because most of the other seats were already filled. I'd always found it funny that even as adults, myself included, people rarely gravitated toward sitting up front unless they had to.

I set my belongings down on a chair and walked over to the elaborate spread of foods. It reminded me of something I'd read in the materials I'd downloaded from the website, that every part of life and work should have a kitchen. If you wanted people to come and participate and share, you had to feed them. This also reminded me of my time in Monaca. There was always something good to eat when our family got together. In fact, all family get-togethers revolved around food. The running joke in the family was that it had been a waste of money to build an entire house because we spent all of our time in Grandma's kitchen. It was the largest room in her small house, and I remember how bright and cheery the yellow flowered wallpaper made everything appear. All the siblings and cousins used to challenge each other for a seat at the gray Formica-topped table with grooved, stainless-steel trim. But as kids, we were at the bottom of the pecking order, so our time at the table was short-lived. We'd always be told to go play and make room for one adult or another. More often than not, however, if we wanted to stay, someone's lap was available.

I filled a plate with some whole-grain toast and fruit, made myself a cup of tea, grabbed a bottle of water, and returned to my seat. I was thinking that the muffins and bagels looked really good, but the one thing I had managed to maintain since leaving Rutter was my fitness routine. I had lost seventeen pounds over the past five months, and I still had ten more to go. Knowing that those last ten pounds were going to be the hardest to lose, I needed to stay committed. Making healthy choices in the face of fresh muffins wasn't easy, but I was determined not to go back to my old habits.

I was surprised to see so many people in attendance. It looked like there were at least one hundred people. Many were chatting in groups, and I assumed that their respective companies had sent them together. I, on the other hand, had taken a sick day to attend, for fear of reprisal. I did a quick scan of the room to see if there was anyone who would know me. It looked like I was safe.

Sitting in my front-row seat, I listened to bits and pieces of conversation. "This is the fourth seminar put on by this presenter that I've attended in the last year," said one of the women who sat behind me. She and her friend were talking to a small group next to them about the positive impact that previous seminars had had on their work and personal lives. "I like to come to this series of seminars because so far at each one, I have taken away at least one thing that inspired me to make a positive change in my life," recalled another woman in the group. "These workshops are part of the Focus LifeStyle[1] series, and they always seem to deliver the tools necessary to turn workshop philosophies into actions," she continued. "I hate it when I attend a workshop and get all jazzed up about the concepts presented and then walk away with no idea about how to integrate them into my life!" The group laughed in unison, and I found myself chuckling as well. How true was that sentiment?

Another small group of men and women was trying to figure out how all of the presentation props were going to be used. Some people had been handed rocks like the one I had been given, and others had been given small packets of sand or pebbles. There were even some walking around with miniature pitchers of water. Everyone had been told to hold on to their props until they were given further instructions. It sure made for some interesting conversations among the participants as they tried to guess what these materials were going to be used for. I heard one man joke that this was probably just a setup and that in a few moments we'd all be ushered onto a bus so we could build a pond in the presenter's backyard—and we'd be paying *him* to do it!

Straining to hear, I faced in another direction and began to listen in on some other conversations. Another group of attendees was discussing their jobs and lives. Based on the conversations I overheard, it was obvious that there was a broad range of professions represented in this room.

At the front of the room on a small stage sat a single medium-sized rectangular table. A black tablecloth with red trim was draped over it. There were some boxes and containers alongside the table filled with contents I couldn't quite see. Two large pitchers of water were being put out. I chuckled to myself and thought, "If we're not building a pond, then this guy must get really thirsty during the presentation. Or maybe he just talks a lot." I began to wonder what I'd really signed up for.

Apparently, I wasn't the only one wondering what was going on; the noise level in the room grew as people spoke among themselves about what was going on, all the while eating their breakfasts as they waited for the seminar to begin. The noise sounded a lot like the family gatherings I remembered in Monaca.

The 9 A.M. start time was drawing near, and the last-minute arrivals were shuffling in quickly at the back of the room, then trying to slink quietly up to the front to fill in the few remaining seats. I looked around for the presenter. So far I'd only met the greeter, whose name was Bill, but I preferred calling him the "Rock Guy." I knew it was just a matter of time before I met the guy Tom had been so excited about.

Right on time at 9 A.M., the doors in the back of the room were closed and the lights were dimmed slightly. "Good morning, everyone, and welcome!" said a loud, confident voice. I turned and quickly realized that the voice belonged to the Rock Guy! I was a little surprised. I wasn't expecting the presenter himself to be the one who greeted the seminar participants with rocks, pebbles, and sand at the door. At the same time, I thought it was kind of cool because, for me, it had set the tone of the seminar as less formal than others I'd been to. There didn't seem to be the typical kind of atmosphere, where all of us bourgeoisie would sit in our chairs waiting for the all-knowing presenter to bestow his amazing knowledge on us. It was more of a "we're all in this together" atmosphere. "That's different," I thought.

"Thanks for taking the time to participate in today's seminar," said the presenter. "I trust that everyone has had a chance to have a bite to eat and settle in for today's BIG ROCKS lifestyle seminar. My name is Dr. Bill Conley; please call me Bill. I am the CEO of an education and training company. I hope you're ready to begin balancing your lives and are ready to have some fun."

"Fun?" I thought. I couldn't remember the last time I could have described a workshop as "fun." I had been thinking about just how desperate I must be to actually attend a workshop like this on my own—without a company sponsor—and now this guy said it was going to be fun? We'd have to see about that!

Following his brief introduction, Bill moved to stand behind the table with the black tablecloth. He pulled a large glass bowl out from underneath the table and centered it on the table. Next, he picked up six good-sized rocks and set them on the table next to the bowl. He held one up to show the audience. "Similar to the rocks I handed each of you when you arrived, I have six big rocks here on the table. Could I ask for a volunteer from the audience to help me with this next part, please?" said Bill.

Because I was in the front of the room, I volunteered. No one was more surprised than I was. I hadn't been in much of a volunteering mood lately.

"Thank you, sir. What is your name and what do you do?" asked Bill.

"Jack, Jack Bedford. I'm an equities manager for a large financial services institution." I quickly scanned the audience, certain someone would yell out, "Hey! You called in sick this morning. What are you doing here?" Fortunately, the room remained silent.

"Okay, Jack. If you are an equities manager, I assume that you are detail oriented and good at following directions. Let's see if you can help me out by following my directions."

I nodded, smiled, and said, "Well, I'll certainly do my best."

"That's the best anyone could hope for!" Bill said with a smile. "Now, I am going to ask you to perform a series of tasks. After I ask you to perform each task, I am going to ask you a question. Before you answer it on your own, I would like for you to solicit help from your fellow workshop attendees and then give me the answer based on what the majority of the audience agrees to, okay?"

"Okay, sounds easy enough," I said.

"Let's begin," said Bill. "What I would like you to do is to place each one of those six big rocks in that large bowl in the center of the table." I did as I was instructed and fitted each rock into the bowl in the most efficient way I could. As soon as all six were settled in the bowl, Bill asked me if the bowl was full. I followed Bill's previous directions by looking to the audience and yelling, "Is it full?" Very quickly the group determined that the bowl was *not* full.

"Okay, Jack," said Bill. He reached for one of the containers alongside the table and lifted it up onto the table. It looked somewhat heavy, and I wondered what was inside as Bill removed the lid.

"Inside this container are lots of small pebbles," Bill continued. "I would like you to empty them into the bowl along with the big rocks."

I emptied the pebbles into the bowl and then tipped the bowl back and forth to even out the pebbles. Once they settled into place among the six big rocks, Bill again asked me if the bowl was full. I again looked to the audience and yelled, "Is it full now?" The group collectively agreed that the bowl was still *not* full.

Bill pulled out yet another container and removed the lid. "This bowl is full of sand," Bill explained to the audience. "Now, Jack, could you please empty the sand into the bowl?"

I proceeded to empty the sand into the mix and leveled out the contents of the bowl. The contents were reaching toward the top. Again, Bill asked the same question: "Is the bowl full now?"

I turned and raised my eyebrows to the audience. This time I didn't bother to ask the question because everyone knew what it was. Several people said yes, the bowl was full. However, the majority agreed that it wasn't. At this point, Bill picked up the large pitchers of water and asked me to fill the bowl without allowing any of the contents to spill over. At least now I knew what all this water was for. I did as I was instructed and poured the water in very carefully.

"Is the bowl full *now?*" asked Bill.

I turned to the audience, and people's shouts and nods determined an agreement that yes, the bowl was now definitely full.

"That's great. I would like to thank you, Jack, for your help. How about a big ripple for Jack, everyone," exclaimed Bill, leading the crowd in an eruption of applause.

I returned to my seat thinking that I had gotten more applause for filling a bowl with dirt than I had for adding a million dollars in equities investments to my company's portfolio last month.

"Now, everyone in this room has watched Jack follow my directions and put all of these contents into the bowl," Bill said. "Is anyone willing to take a stab at figuring out the point of this demonstration?"

The room was silent. Many people were looking down or off to the side, hoping they wouldn't be called on to answer this question. Bill looked around the room and waited patiently.

I was relieved to know that I wouldn't be expected to answer because I'd already volunteered for filling the bowl. It's almost an unspoken rule in meetings or workshops that once you've volunteered, nothing else is expected from you, for a little while anyway.

No one wanted to reply for fear of giving the wrong answer. I thought how well we adults had learned in school not to risk speaking and being wrong. Finally, a woman in the middle of the crowd seated across from me spoke. "It takes an awful lot of stuff to fill up a bowl?" she replied uncertainly.

"You're right about that!" said Bill. "Good start. That's definitely true. Now, let's see if I can help by asking a more specific question. You all saw me put six rocks into the bowl. If you came to this workshop because the title was 'BIG ROCKS: Balancing Work and Life,' what do you think the six big rocks might represent?"

There was another long pause, and Bill again waited patiently. I noticed that he didn't call on anyone to answer. He was giving us time to think things through. I wondered if this was deliberate. Just as I was trying to answer that question in my own head, a woman to Bill's right responded.

"Well, when you ask the question that way, it becomes clear to me that the big rocks you put into the bowl represent the most important aspects of a person's life. I am guessing that the pebbles, sand, and water are all the extra stuff we would rather not have to contend with."

"Fantastic," replied Bill. "You are right. I like to think of the big rocks as a person's true life priorities. Let me ask you this: Why do you think I put the six big rocks in first?"

"Based on the contents that are in that bowl now, I guess you put them in first because there would be no way to get them in later without making a big mess," the woman said.

Just as she was finishing her answer, Bill picked up another rock and tried to fit it into the bowl. The water, sand, and pebbles quickly came spilling down the sides of the bowl and onto the table. "Is this what you mean?" asked Bill. Heads around the room bobbed up and down in agreement. It seemed as though participants were beginning to understand.

That certainly was a good example of *my* life, I thought. One big bowl of overflowing chaos!

"Now, I detected a hint of sarcasm in your response, which is good because I like the humor, but you are exactly right," said Bill. "If we put our big rocks into the bowl last, they wouldn't fit. The point of this hands-on demonstration is that if you want to achieve balance in your life, you need to put your BIG ROCKS in first and attend to them accordingly. I tried to fit one more big rock into this bowl, and I made a big mess on purpose. Isn't that what most of us do in our lives? We try to put the things most important to us in last, and then we feel out of balance when they don't fit. Putting them in last upsets the balance.

"Magic. Well done. Now, let me ask you another question. Why do you think I only put six big rocks into the bowl? Why didn't I put ten or twelve?"

After a brief silence, a man to my left spoke up. "Well if you put ten or twelve into the bowl, you wouldn't have been able to fit the sand, pebbles, and water."

"Good answer," said Bill. "Can anyone else add to that and give me other reasons why I only put six big rocks into the bowl?"

More people were starting to get involved. I noticed that eight or nine hands were up now, and Bill was taking a bit of time to choose which person he wanted to call on. I think that this is what is referred to as "working the room." Finally, he called on a woman in the back.

"Well, if you're trying to balance your life and the big rocks represent the most important things in your life, then having more than six rocks, or important things, may be too difficult to balance," she replied, growing more confident in her answer as it came out of her mouth.

Bill said, "You are exactly right. My experience in teaching the BIG

ROCKS strategy has shown that trying to handle more than six important things or priorities in your life at once is typically too overwhelming for most of us to achieve successfully.

"Now, let me relate this to your lives. Do most of you feel on a daily basis that you are trying to cram in the things that are most important to you at the last minute—just like I demonstrated when I tried to fit that seventh rock into the bowl and all the other contents came spilling out? The sand, pebbles, and water represent all of the things that are necessary but are not your BIG ROCKS, yet they take up the majority of your time. We are constantly trying to jam our priorities—or our BIG ROCKS—into our lives before we've adequately made enough room for them. I have the same issues that you do, and it's frustrating. We are all trying to find balance, and it is the main reason why you came to this workshop today!"

I felt like I was starting to catch on. Bill was basically making two main points. First, I needed to identify my priorities, and second, I needed to find a way to put them into my own bowl first. He was right. I was always trying to put my biggest priorities into my bowl last.

I looked around and noticed that Bill had everyone's full attention. People were leaning forward in their seats, and by their interested looks I realized that prioritizing the important things in life must not be only my problem. It seemed like a lot of them were also struggling—looking for a way back to a simpler life.

Bill continued, "Although we've mentioned the sand, pebbles, and water, can anyone give me specific examples of what these items represent?"

Bill didn't have to wait for responses this time. They came at him rapid-fire. People were shouting out answers, eager to be heard. I heard answers such as "My job," "My hobbies," "Travel," "Dry cleaning," "Grocery shopping," "Shuffling my kids around to all of their activities," and so on. One woman shouted, "My weight-loss program." Her response received many smiles, and many heads around the room were nodding in empathy with that issue.

I noticed that people were starting to open up now and risk sharing personal information about their lives. I was sure that this was what Bill was trying to accomplish by getting us to create the responses that were meaningful to our own lives.

Workshop participants continued to provide more answers, and Bill patiently listened and nodded. As the responses died out, he continued,

"Without going into great detail at this point in time, the sand, the pebbles, and the water represent everything that you just said. Fitting those things together with your BIG ROCKS creates balance. A balanced life leads to fulfilled individuals and a healthy lifestyle."

As I looked around the room, I realized I was nodding in unison with many others. Bill was opening my eyes to what I already knew was important. The things I needed to do to balance my life were so simple when I looked at them from this perspective, yet I wasn't doing them. I didn't know why I wasn't doing these things consistently. I really didn't have an answer, but I guessed that was why I was here.

SIX

Believing: The BIG ROCKS Philosophy

After a brief pause, Bill resumed the workshop by glancing around the room at all of us in the audience.

"As I look at all of you, I see in most of your eyes the duality of your understanding of the simplicity of the concept behind the BIG ROCKS activity. On one hand, you are all making the connection between how the rocks, pebbles, sand, and water relate to your own lives. It's obvious by your expressions and your body language that you get it. On the other hand, I sense that you are now wondering why you are not living a balanced life if the solution is as plain and simple as I have just pointed out. If it's so simple, why are you not living your life's true priorities? Why are you here trying to figure it out for yourselves?"

He asked, "Am I reaching anyone here? Am I tapping into how anyone is feeling about their lives?"

Hands went up, and many participants were nodding to signal their understanding. Bill called on a man sitting off to the left, alone, in the back of the room with his arms crossed over his chest. As the noise quieted down, Bill called out, "Sir, sitting in the back in the red shirt, you look frustrated; do you have another opinion?"

"Umm, well, I was just thinking that I do connect with what you're saying. I guess I look frustrated because I am. I don't know why I can't balance everything. It's a good question." The man paused for a breath and then continued, "I'm thirty-eight years old, and I have four children. I'd like to think that I am fairly intelligent and a relatively successful businessman. I provide well for my family. We have a nice house and a comfortable life. Yet these issues that you refer to as 'fitting it all in' have been dogging me for the past five years or so."

"Tell me more about that," urged Bill. "What do you mean by 'dogging you'?"

"Well, for starters, I work too much. On average I put in about sixty to seventy hours per week, and my boss continues to pressure me to do more. Because of this, my wife and kids are neglected. They feel left out of my life. And I have to be honest; my energy level is low when I get home late at night. I find the demands from my wife and kids to be overwhelming at times because I am so tired, and I just need some time for myself. Then the guilt sets in because there isn't even enough time for my wife and kids, never mind me. My wife faces the same pressures. She works, too. All of this weighs heavily on our relationship. If you were to examine my life in more detail, Bill, you would find that I am truly the poster child for what you call being 'out of balance.' I am tired, frustrated, and unable to continue at this pace. Well, I shouldn't say 'unable.' Unwilling is more like it. I need to make some changes for my own sanity. There's nothing but quicksand in my bowl, and I'm sinking in it."

"Excuse me, sir, what's your name?" asked Bill.

"Joe McFarlane."

"Thanks, Joe. First, let me say thanks for sharing that information with the group, and second, let me say that you are at the right workshop because the information I am going to present to you today will get you on your way to making those necessary changes in your life. There is a light at the end of the tunnel.

"Now, let me ask another question of all of you. Does Joe speak for many of you? Does his story resonate?" Nearly all of the heads in the room nodded in agreement. The particulars changed from person to person, yet the underlying story remained the same.

"All right, I think everyone is making the connection with the metaphor of BIG ROCKS, and hopefully I am gaining some believers in the philosophy. So at this point, I would like to continue by asking you all to refer to the workbooks that you were handed as you signed in this morning. Please turn to the first page," Bill said as he put the same question that was in our books up on the screen. "I would like you to consider the following question and write down your answer to it in your packets."

Write down JUST ONE lifestyle choice you could put into action AT WORK that you know would bring about positive results.

"I'll give everyone a few minutes to write a response in your booklet."

I considered the question for a minute and then began to write out my response: *"Communicate my needs more clearly—be specific—and take more responsibility for getting them met."*

"Great," said Bill as he changed the image. "Now, let's consider another question. Again, I would like everyone to take a few minutes and write down a response."

Write down JUST ONE lifestyle choice you could put into action in your PERSONAL LIFE that you know would bring about positive results.

I considered the question for a minute. It seemed so simple, but coming up with a single answer wasn't that easy. There were probably many things I should be doing, but I wasn't sure which one should be at the top of the list. After several more minutes I finally wrote, *"To honor my commitments to my wife and children 99.9 percent of the time. To be there for things that are important to them and always let them know that they come first."*

Again Bill paused for several minutes and then asked, "Is everyone finished?" He scanned the room and waited until the last few people gave him their full attention, signaling that everyone had written responses to his questions. "Great. Now I have one more question for you. I need all eyes up on the screen because I would like you to read it for yourself. This is the most difficult question of the three, and I want you to really think about the answer."

In bold black letters the following question was staring me in the face:

IF YOU KNOW THESE ACTIONS WOULD RESULT IN MORE POSITIVE OUTCOMES IN BOTH YOUR PERSONAL AND PROFESSIONAL LIVES, WHY AREN'T YOU DOING THEM NOW?

Everyone looked stumped. That certainly was an epiphany question. I hoped he didn't really expect us to answer it.

After a few moments, Bill asked, "Is it safe to assume that everyone wrote something down for the first two questions?"

The audience responded, "Yes."

"What does that tell us?"

"That we all made it to the right workshop," someone called from the middle of the crowd. This pulled out a few chuckles from the group.

"Yes, that's true," Bill said with a knowing grin. "But what else does that tell us?" He looked around for someone to respond. When it appeared as though no one was ready to answer, he continued before allowing silence to fill the room.

"I believe that the two key issues we are dealing with in this workshop are **balance** and **alignment.** I believe that these are the most significant issues affecting individuals, families, and organizations today. I used to believe that it was only a problem that we experienced here in the Western world, but I now know that it is more universal.

"I've already explained the concept of balance to you with the BIG ROCKS demonstration. Alignment goes hand in hand with balance. Alignment happens when individuals are able to get their thoughts, feelings, and actions consistent within themselves and with those around them.[1] People that I have trained in the past have defined alignment as 'life's equilibrium.' Before I get ahead of myself, let's get back to the metaphor of BIG ROCKS, and I will explain more about alignment later.

"Now that you understand the metaphor of BIG ROCKS, I would like to spend just a few minutes sharing some of my background with you, and how it has come to be that I am standing here before you. It will help build your picture of the importance of what you'll be learning today.

"For over thirty years now I have worked to build my own businesses and found that the key to success was learning to grow my people alongside the products and services I was offering. As an entrepreneur, I didn't start out knowing this, but, rather, I stumbled onto that lesson. It was a combination of instinct, luck, perseverance, and a lot of hard work. I learned that by meeting the needs of the people within my organization, business success surely followed.[2]

"Meeting the needs of all the people within my organization, however, is not as easily done as it is said. Human beings easily veer off track in their lives or find themselves 'out of alignment.' To meet the needs of my people, I took on the responsibility of teaching my employees to recognize when they are out of alignment and, in turn, make a correction. Making a correction always came back to revisiting an individual's BIG ROCKS and pulling them, once again, to the forefront of that person's life. Remember, it is about defining the priorities or BIG ROCKS specific to us, keeping those priorities at the fore-

front of how we plan and manage our time, and being diligent about eliminating interference along the way.

"I'm going to explain further why I chose to begin today's workshop with
the BIG ROCKS activity, and what it had to do with balancing the most
important things or true priorities of your lives. The BIG ROCKS that were
handed to you as you entered this room today, and the ones we used to put
into the bowl for the demonstration, represent the major priorities in your
lives. They should be the most important things in your life. For example,
my BIG ROCKS are my wife, my children, my work, and my personal well-
being. Those are my major priorities, and whenever I am confronted with
decisions in my own life, I take into consideration how those decisions affect
each one of my BIG ROCKS. I then work to eliminate any interference that
can take away from my priorities.

"Now, for those of you who were handed pebbles, sand, or small pitchers
of water when you arrived, understand that all of those items represent interference. I want to be clear that some interference is in fact necessary; however, some of it is not. This is why I will teach you how to sort out the necessary from the unnecessary interference and eliminate the unnecessary.

"I make very conscious choices about how I allocate my time," said Bill.
"If you look again at our bowl, you will notice that the pebbles, sand, and
water all represent interference. You must understand that there is always
room to fit more into your lives, but not always with good results. No one
here wanted to stop with putting just the big rocks into the bowl. You all said
it wasn't full. You could have chosen to say it was full after the pebbles were
put in, or after the sand was added, but this group wanted the bowl to be
fuller. After you leave this workshop today, you may want to rethink your
definition of 'full.' Stop overwhelming yourself—it's not necessary. Maybe
five big rocks and some pebbles will be full enough for you and help you
achieve balance, because when fitting in more begins to take away from your
BIG ROCKS, or knocks them out of your bowl, it's time to think about
attaining more balance and refocusing on the priorities that you have defined
as specific to you.

"Think about what would happen if I had continued to add more and
more water, sand, and pebbles to the point where the bowl overflowed and
eventually started pushing out the big rocks. Is that what anyone really wants
to do? Do you really want to push your BIG ROCKS out of the bowl? Of
course you don't. And that's very clear when you are looking at it in the lit-

eral sense. However, many of us push our BIG ROCKS out of our lives every day by allowing too much interference into our lives. So today, I am going to show you how to refocus and find balance. Once I teach you the secret to finding balance and provide you with the tools you need, keep them handy to continuously work on maintaining balance in your lives every day."

"Excuse me, Bill," mumbled an older man sitting directly behind me. "Isn't the BIG ROCKS strategy really about time management? That's what it's sounding like to me."

"You are absolutely right. Yet I want you to recognize that time management is only one factor, not the major issue. I learned a long time ago that if balancing lives was as easy as managing everyone's time, I could simply hand you all a watch. Time management, in the traditional sense of how it was defined in the mid- to late '80s, is flawed. We will address time management as a factor of the BIG ROCKS strategy; however, we need to focus on the issue, which I've identified as balance and alignment. To achieve successful balance and alignment in our lives, we need to eliminate interference.

"Up until now, I haven't fully explained interference. Simply put, it is the difference between where we want to be and where we believe we are. Interference is really whatever in your life is blocking you from nurturing your true priorities. I often use radio static as an analogy. Has anyone ever tried to listen to a really great song on the radio, and there was static interfering with the clarity of the sound?"

Everyone gave an understanding nod.

"Well, if there was static, what would be the first thing you would do?" questioned Bill.

"I would try to tune in the station better to get a clearer sound," responded a woman in the middle of the room.

"Exactly," said Bill. "You would try to gain some clarity, which is what you need to do to eliminate interference. Implementing the BIG ROCKS strategy can be as simple as the fine-tuning you do with your radio, except you are fine-tuning your life. Some of you may need just a slight adjustment, whereas others may need to adjust your stations with a full 180-degree turn of the dial. I hope that many of you are beginning to gain some clarity right now.

"Think back to the BIG ROCKS demonstration. I think we all understand that some sand, pebbles, and water are necessary. However, later on you will discover that the balance between those three things and your BIG ROCKS is the key to the success of this strategy. You must take ownership for identifying and managing the priorities unique to your life. You must make the effort to put them first. Remember, you cannot control what life presents you, but you can choose to control how you deal with it.

"Now, this morning, as I reviewed the information sheets about each of you, I recognized that everyone here today works for some type of organization. I think it is important to note that even people who don't have a paid job, per se, are still involved with organizations. It may be the organization of your home and/or family, or organizations that you serve through volunteer work or charities. What this means is that all of us have multiple aspects of our lives that we need to balance. I mention this because some of you may have spouses or significant others at home whom you wish to involve in the BIG ROCKS strategy. I want to make sure that everyone recognizes that 'work' doesn't have to mean paid employment. It could just as easily mean managing the children or volunteering for an organization that someone is passionate about."

As I looked around I noticed nearly everyone nodding in agreement, and many participants were leaning forward in their seats waiting to hear more.

"Let's take a moment to talk about organizations. Today's BIG ROCKS workshop is slightly different for me because I typically conduct these workshops within specific organizations, and one of the goals is to get people in the same work environment to implement this strategy together. Another goal is team-building. Today, however, I have many of you here that are from different organizations, so during this workshop I will be individualizing the strategy as well as providing you with useful tips that will help you share this with your respective organizations. Some of you may also choose to use this within your families, and that's fantastic because I believe that one of the many great things about the BIG ROCKS strategy is its flexibility.

"Meeting the needs of everyone within an organization is not an easy thing to do. It requires constant attention because people's needs vary widely and change over time. Just look at the volumes of business-oriented literature written over the past twenty years pertaining to adequately meeting the needs of employees to enhance productivity and boost morale. Let me give you an example.

"How many of you have been praised for a job well done over the past two weeks?[3] If you have been praised over the past two weeks, put your hand up."

Bill scanned the room, and there wasn't a single hand up. Maybe it was just me, but I thought people were even sinking down in their seats for effect. I kept my hand down because the only praise I had received was insincere. I didn't believe that counted.

Bill continued, "Let me ask you this question. How many of you in here would have liked to have been praised over the past two weeks?" Bill scanned the room once again. This time nearly everyone's hand was raised high. "Exactly," said Bill. "You see, the issue isn't that we don't know that people want to be praised; the issue is that we don't know how or why to praise people. Research from the Gallup Institute's productive culture survey reveals that employee praise needs to happen at least once every seven days to meet the minimum commitment of what we all need in terms of praise and recognition. It is a basic human need, but we don't meet it often enough.

"Over the past ten to thirty years most companies' focus has been on the bottom line. In fact, it may even be more predominant today than ever before. The focus hasn't been on the people within an organization but rather on money and productivity. I think organizations have slowly begun to realize that people are important to the success of their business. Until recently, we haven't had any evidence to support the idea that if you don't treat your people right, you are not going to gain the greatest amount of productivity from each individual. Now that we have that research available, let me share with you some additional research from the Gallup Institute."

An image appeared on the screen, a globe with statistics from various countries surrounding it.

"The only thing that we have had in the past to concretely measure the success of any organization has been a balance sheet. Although it is, in fact, a solid indicator of business success, it is also a lag indicator, meaning that we learn after the fact how we have done. Also, it doesn't measure all aspects of organizational success. How much productivity are you actually getting out of people? Are they working to their fullest capacity or potential? This chart I am sharing with you was compiled from research and is basically a way to measure the potential for organizational success.

"The statistics reflected in this research are disappointing. Look at the number of people that are disengaged from their work in the countries

GLOBAL STATISTICS ON EMPLOYEE ENGAGEMENT

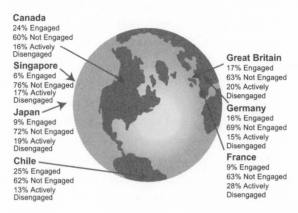

Canada
24% Engaged
60% Not Engaged
16% Actively
Disengaged

Singapore
6% Engaged
76% Not Engaged
17% Actively
Disengaged

Japan
9% Engaged
72% Not Engaged
19% Actively
Disengaged

Chile
25% Engaged
62% Not Engaged
13% Actively
Disengaged

Great Britain
17% Engaged
63% Not Engaged
20% Actively
Disengaged

Germany
16% Engaged
69% Not Engaged
15% Actively
Disengaged

France
9% Engaged
63% Not Engaged
28% Actively
Disengaged

SOURCE: GALLUP ORGANIZATION

depicted on the graph. To provide perspective, in the United States, 74 percent of our workforce admits to not being engaged or being actively disengaged.[4] Can you begin to imagine how productivity could be enhanced if we could only reengage the disengaged?"

An attendee interrupted Bill to ask, "You mean to tell me that the same companies that are successful in financial terms are unsuccessful in terms of employee engagement?"

"That's correct, but it also means that there is significant room for improvement. These are good companies that are willing to accept being 'good enough.' Other industry research from Jim Collins that is outlined in his book *Good to Great* suggests that good is actually the evil nemesis of great. Once companies achieve an adequate level of financial success, they become complacent by leveraging only these lag indicators. What I am showing you with this chart are *lead indicators*. Lead indicators provide an understanding of whether or not the group of people working in any organization is poised and willing to drive the company in the direction that meets both the company's vision and its financial projections.[5] If we can understand and implement the concept of engagement, we can predict both future individual and organizational success. As Jim Collins would say, 'We can take good companies and make them great.'

"Let me explain what the Gallup Institute has found in its long-term research surrounding employee engagement. As you'll notice on the screen, there are numbers that represent various countries and their percentages of engagement and disengagement. These are the researched levels of engagement for people working in an organization.

"Engagement measures the level of emotional attachment that an employee has to his coworkers and/or organization. What Gallup has found is that the higher the level of engagement, the better the person feels about himself as an individual and about the organization he is a part of. Because of this, he works harder, feels better, and overall feels as though he is winning. Moreover, this is where organizations win, too. When an employee is happier, or more fulfilled, that employee becomes more productive. You should realize that this has an effect on balance. The more an individual feels good about who he is and where he works, the easier it is for him to balance his life. However, engagement is only half of the solution in the fulfillment of balance. I believe the other half is alignment.

"Alignment, according to ongoing research and analysis from the Focus Group Limited, goes beyond being emotionally engaged. Alignment has more to do with groups of people than individuals. However, in order to align any group of people, we must first begin with aligning each individual in the group. It is exactly what I am doing with all of you as a group today. Those of you who succeed in balancing your lives will find that it has a positive effect on the groups of people you surround yourselves with—whether that be family members, friends, or coworkers.

"The reality is that it is normal and natural to be out of alignment at various times in your life. However, what many people struggle with is knowing how to get themselves back into alignment, or how to get their lives back into balance. If you are unable to do that, you will ultimately feel as though your life is out of control. What the BIG ROCKS workshop will do for you is give you back the control you crave.

"As it relates to a work environment, the principle of alignment is the same. People working within any group can go out of alignment. Organizationally speaking, alignment gets everyone in the organization thinking in the same manner, feeling committed in the same way, and working toward the same goals. BIG ROCKS is just one component of alignment.

"Let me give you a simple example of alignment. Have you ever walked out of a meeting thinking you knew exactly what was expected of you? You began tackling the task according to the expectations that came out of that meeting. Then someone came over and asked what you were doing, and when you told them, they said, 'No that's not what you were supposed to do!'"

Heads around the room nodded, and several chuckles escaped from participants.

"Some of you may be sitting there asking yourselves, 'Why does he keep going on about engagement and alignment?' I understand that I have more to explain, and I promise it will become clearer as we move forward in this workshop. However, understanding engagement and alignment is vital to the success of the BIG ROCKS strategy.

"One of the most significant outcomes of engagement and alignment is employee retention. An engaged and aligned individual is one whom an organization retains. This is key because the average rate of retention for businesses around the globe today is 3.4 years.[6] Can anyone imagine how much money businesses could save by retaining employees as opposed to constantly having to pay to train new ones? The cost of continually losing employees over time is exorbitant. Today's businesses have moved to the opposite extreme of what they used to be years ago. Think back to the era your parents or grandparents grew up in, depending upon your age. It wasn't uncommon for that generation of people to join an organization straight out of school and stay with it for their entire careers. Today this is the exception, not the rule. Today's workforce is nomadic, moving from job to job. In fact, Richard Sennett, a sociologist at New York University, has calculated that a young American today with at least two years of college can expect to change jobs eleven times before retirement.[7] As a result of the revolving door of employees moving in and out of organizations, those organizations are typically found to be out of alignment or out of balance because there is too much transition. Organizations are failing to recognize the significant impact that too many employee changes can have on everything from their morale to their bottom line.

"Since 1950, society has changed dramatically. Back then, people lived to work, and it was typical for people to maintain their jobs over a lifetime. There were fewer choices then. We worked because we needed to make ends meet. Often we worked multiple jobs just to meet our basic needs and provide for our families. Today is radically different. Today we work to live. Today many people work to live chosen lifestyles that stretch beyond satisfying basic needs into accommodating more costly wants. We want more than just making ends meet. We want to take advantage of all that life has to offer and enjoy our lives to the fullest, including time for our loved ones, friends, travel, varying interests, and multiple careers.

"Many societies around the world have done well to create an abundance of opportunities to elevate the quality of life for individuals. This increase has resulted in the availability of a greater number of choices within these societies, and while that is an incredible achievement in and of itself because our world is better able to meet the needs of many, rather than only an elite few, it has also created new challenges. This shift has left people with lives that are full but oftentimes not fulfilled.

"Consider a child at a typical candy counter today with the abundance of choices that are common. If you tell the child to pick one item, he will usually have difficulty choosing just one because there are too many choices. The abundance of choice makes the decision too complex.

"Even as adults, the abundance of choice can overwhelm us, leaving us paralyzed or unable to decide and focus on just one thing. It is a blessing to have so many choices, but we as human beings must now learn how to manage the prioritization of the choices available to us. (Identify your BIG ROCKS.) We need to be realistic about how much we can actually take advantage of at any given point in out lives. (How full do we fill our own bowls?) Most of us try to do too much all at once. We must learn how to focus on the most important choices and then be decisive and confident in making them productive choices for ourselves. (When do we schedule actions related to our choices into our lives?)

"The added pressure of so many available choices has opened the door to another subset of societal issues. We would think that the newfound abundance of choice in our world today would have created a sense of calm and increased wellness among all human beings. If that is so, then how do we explain why we can't build prisons fast enough? Why are there so many adults and children relying on medications such as Prozac and Ritalin just to make it through the day? Why are suicide rates soaring among college students? Why have so many Americans become overweight to the point that obesity is now classified as an epidemic and a disease?

"The list of these types of questions is long. Logic would tell us that amidst so much prosperity and opportunity, these issues would lessen, yet it is not the case. Although all of these issues are acute and must be addressed directly, BIG ROCKS does not focus on these symptomatic issues. BIG

ROCKS aims to reveal the larger challenge, or the root cause that is chronically affecting so many of us: the issue of balance.

"Implementing BIG ROCKS challenges you to take a serious look at what you need to do differently in your personal and professional lives to achieve a greater degree of balance and personal fulfillment. I will restate once again that time is not the issue. If it were, I'd hand everyone a watch and say, 'Thanks for coming.' Speaking of watches, why don't we all take a fifteen-minute break to stretch, fill our coffee cups, or have a snack?"

SEVEN

BIG ROCKS TOOL BOX 1:

BIG ROCK
Identification

A s my fellow workshop participants began to get up and move away from their seats, I walked over to refill my cup of tea and get some fruit. I carried the tea with the fruit balanced on top over to a small table at the back of the room. I noticed that several others were doing the same, and before long my attention had tuned in to a group discussion between three people who I assumed were colleagues and their thoughts on this workshop so far. They invited me to join them.

"The engagement statistic was interesting to me," said a short, dark-haired man. "I find it ironic that Japan is reporting one of the highest numbers for employees that are disengaged. For years, American businesses have pointed to Japanese workers as a model of productivity and teamwork. The Japanese prided themselves on Total Quality Management (TQM)."[1]

"Maybe, like Bill said, there was just too much focus on the bottom line and not enough focus on the human capital within organizations. It sounds like overworked, underappreciated, and disengaged!" chimed in the woman standing next to him. Her name was Tara.

"I'm just amazed that we are actually measuring this now, and it is something that is important enough to be researched by an organization like Gallup," added a man with the name "Paul" written on his nametag. "It's nice to know that someone actually cares about the people working within the organization rather than just caring about the organization and its bottom line."

"I don't think that it is so much about organizations not caring," continued Tara. "All organizations claim to care, and I'm sure they do. The difference is that most organizations don't back up the fact that they care with any actions that reflect the caring!"

"Well said," added the second woman, whose nametag I couldn't quite read. "Isn't it also amazing that the engagement factor is now tied to employee retention? Think about what Bill said about past generations. John, I know that your grandfather worked for the phone company for forty-something years. My grandfather worked for the local bank for forty-six years."

"He's right," I said. "I think he summed it up perfectly when he said that it used to be that people lived to work, and now we work to live."

The others nodded in agreement. I finished my fruit and tea and made my way back to my seat. I sat down and organized my materials, looked over my notes, and jotted down a few additional thoughts that I'd taken from the discussion during the break. I was taking in a lot of information, and I wanted to make sure I didn't forget it when I left. Just as I was finishing, I looked up to see Bill making his way to the front of the room again. I relaxed into my seat and got ready for the next part of the workshop.

"Welcome back," said Bill. "I hope you've all had a chance to chat with one another briefly about what we've covered so far. I know it was a lot of theory, but my goal is to build the concept and solidify your belief in the BIG ROCKS strategy first. Now we can move on to discussing the most challenging part, which is actively living BIG ROCKS. At this point in the presentation, I am going to give you the actual tools you'll need to live the BIG ROCKS strategy and teach you how to use them."

After scanning the room and listening to the last of multiple conversations trail off, Bill continued.

"Implementing the BIG ROCKS strategy begins with identifying your personal BIG ROCKS. If everyone would turn to the section in your workshop materials titled BIG ROCKS TOOL BOX, you will find a worksheet that provides you spaces to write in your BIG ROCKS. I have provided an example for you to follow. Let's all take a few minutes right now and really think about what the BIG ROCKS are in our lives and write them in the spaces provided. You should have no more than six BIG ROCKS. Depending on how you identify them, you may even have fewer than six BIG ROCKS, and that's perfectly fine."

Activity One

Identify Your Life's Priorities

What are the things in your life that are most important to you? Write in no more than six of the top priorities in your life—your BIG ROCKS.

BIG ROCKS WORKING EXAMPLE

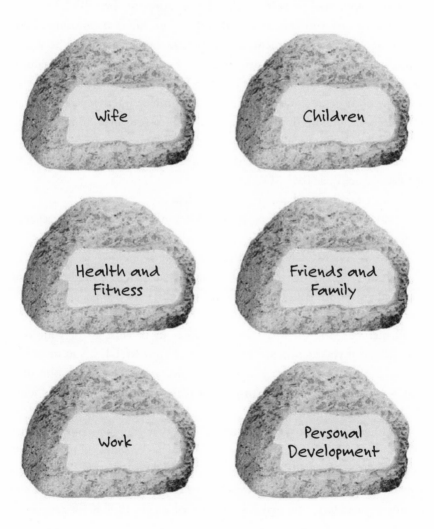

I thought about it for a few minutes and finally identified five BIG ROCKS for myself. The first was my wife, Lisa. The second was my children, Jake and Beckie. The third was my extended family and friends. My fourth was my personal well-being. By that I meant physical fitness and down time for myself. The fifth and final BIG ROCK was my career and work. I checked over the list and tried to think whether there might be another BIG ROCK that I should include, but I ultimately decided that five was a good number for me.

"How is everyone doing?" asked Bill. Heads around the room nodded to signal that they had completed the identification of their BIG ROCKS. "Congratulations, you have all just identified your life's true priorities. Look them over carefully, study them, and memorize them. You should be able to rattle these off to anyone who asks you just as easily as you say your name. I ask that you memorize these BIG ROCKS because when you know what your true priorities are, it becomes easier to eliminate interference, or at least to manage the amount of interference you let into your lives. It makes it easier to achieve balance and move you toward alignment. Would anyone like to share their BIG ROCKS with the group?" Bill chose about eight or nine people to share their BIG ROCKS.

"I chose family," said one man in the back.

"Okay. Did you choose one ROCK for family, or did you use separate ROCKS for individual family members?" asked Bill.

"I just did one ROCK for family. Did I do it wrong?"

"No, that's totally fine. Please understand that there is no right or wrong way to identify your BIG ROCKS. You are all different people, and how you choose to identify your priorities and live by them is up to you.

"Remember, you are the one who needs to balance all of your own ROCKS. So if you identified family as one of your ROCKS, you must balance all of the people whom you consider your family with all of your other ROCKS. As long as you can manage the balance, then your method of identification is right for you.

"Another important point to remember is that your life's priorities may change over time. Not only is it acceptable but it's encouraged to reidentify your BIG ROCKS at different points in your life. For example, some of you may have small children, which we all know requires a great deal of time and attention. Therefore, you may have identified a BIG ROCK for each small child and one for your spouse or significant other. In contrast, some of you may have children who are grown, and therefore, you may have simply identified 'children' or 'family' for your BIG ROCK. Again, it is really about whatever works for you, depending on what your priorities are at this point in your life. There are no right or wrong answers.

"How many of you identified individual members of your family as separate ROCKS?" asked Bill.

About half of the hands in the room went up. "I put down my husband as one of my BIG ROCKS, and I used another single ROCK for each of my three children. Is that okay?" asked a woman sitting in the front.

"Absolutely," said Bill. "Now, what are some of the other BIG ROCKS that have been identified?"

"I put down personal time for myself," said another woman.

"I put down travel or vacation time," said another.

The responses continued to pour out of the audience. "I put down my hobby." "I have fitness as one of my BIG ROCKS." As the answers began to sound more and more similar, Bill looked to find some new responses. "Does anyone have ROCKS that are different from what we've heard so far?"

"I identified my career as one of my BIG ROCKS," said a man in the back of the room. "I haven't heard anyone say that yet."

Bill agreed, "You're right. Career or work isn't typically the first ROCK to be identified. Each person I called on just now identified family, friends, fitness, travel, etc., as their first ROCKS. That's generally what happens.

"Sir, did you identify your career as your first ROCK?" asked Bill. The man said no and told us it was his fourth ROCK.

"Did anyone identify work as one of your top three ROCKS?" Bill asked and scanned the room to see that about 10 percent of the workshop participants had their hands raised. My hand was not among them because I had chosen career as my fifth ROCK.

"I just want everyone to realize that this response is typical of what I see whenever I pose this question to a group of workshop participants. So, did any of you identify work as your top priority, or the first ROCK?"

A handful of people raised their hands cautiously.

"Miss, can you tell us why you identified work as your first-priority ROCK?"

"Well, I'm single, and I don't have any children. I just graduated from college about two years ago, and my main focus has been on building my career," she replied. "It's also been about paying off my college debt. That's another reason why work is so important to me."

"Absolutely; that sounds about right. That priority makes perfect sense for someone living under those circumstances. Back to the point that I was making earlier about priorities changing, let me ask you another question. If in ten years you find yourself married with several children, do you still think that work would be identified as your top priority?"

"I doubt it," said the young woman. "I hope to have my career established to a point where work is part of my life, but not as big a part as it is today. In fact, the reason that I came to this workshop today is because I have been feeling as though work is taking up too much of my time. I want to have more time to do things for myself and create a better social life. Many of my college friends have gotten married and settled down. Their lives have changed, and I don't feel like I fit in with them as well as I used to. We hardly ever have time to get together, and I would like to change that. I guess that I am just at a point where I see that work doesn't have to be everything, and I am looking for some advice and ways to change that about my life."

"I hope that you also identified friends or social life as one of your BIG ROCKS because the tools that I am going to share will help you create time for the things in your life you feel are missing," said Bill. "I also think you make a good point about work taking up too much of your time right now. I would guess that the majority of my participants today are here for the same exact reason you are. Too many corporations and businesses hold strongly to the belief that maximizing the number of hours an employee works results in maximized productivity. It simply isn't true. Maximizing hours eventually leads to diminished productivity, employee resentment, and diminished retention.[2] Others of you are here because you feel work takes up too much of your time, just like our single friend here; you may even have children and spouses and 'bowls' that are even more full than hers. So the fact that this young woman is trying to adopt strategies at this stage of her life is a true credit to her. I'm confident that this workshop can provide the tools to change the lifestyle of anyone here in this room. Your responsibility will be to consistently choose to use the tools," said Bill.

"Is everyone comfortable with understanding that the identification of your priorities is (1) unique to you and (2) dependent upon the circumstances of your life?"

Everyone gave a nod to signal agreement.

"Some of you may have been surprised that work or career is typically not one of the top three ROCKS to be identified by most people. This is what I meant when I told you that today we work in order to live. Living is the first priority in our society, and working is secondary. Fifty years ago, people asked to identify BIG ROCKS would most likely have chosen work as one of their top ROCKS because they had to. Today, things are different. We choose to work because we want a higher standard of living as opposed to having to work to meet the basic needs of our families and ourselves. Most of us are able to meet our own basic needs and those of our families while also enjoying more of our income than others from generations past have. A greater percentage of us have expendable income we can use to enjoy our lives. I know that is not true across the board, but it has certainly improved since 1950 and will hopefully continue to improve.

"Some of you may have not even identified work as a BIG ROCK, which is fine as long as you realize that for the majority of us, work needs to fit in somewhere. If it is not one of *your* BIG ROCKS, it would have to be considered some part of the sand, pebbles, or water in your 'bowls.' For the majority of the population, working is not a choice, and therefore it must be balanced in your lives in some way. People must balance what they *want* to do with what they *have* to do. They must take responsibility for themselves. Don't get me wrong; there are some people who don't take responsibility for balancing work in their lives. These people are generally referred to as 'teenagers.'"

Soft laughter erupted from the workshop participants, and Bill took a moment to take a sip of water before moving on.

"For those of you who are executives or responsible for managing people within organizations, it is very important that you hear what I am telling you right now: work is not a top priority for the majority of people. You would be kidding yourselves if you believed otherwise. Families, friends, and extracurricular activities are most people's priorities. Those are the most important BIG ROCKS for just about everyone. Those are the ROCKS that reenergize us and typically bring the most joy into our lives. Families and friends are the people from whom we draw our strength. And the reason we often feel so out of balance is because it is this ROCK that is most often neglected and pushed out of the bowl by interference. I'm not saying that people don't want their work to have meaning; they absolutely do. When work doesn't have meaning, people will leave their jobs in search of something that is more personally fulfilling. Just as people seek to find fulfillment in their personal lives, they also seek to find fulfillment in their professional lives. Furthermore, when you do find meaning in your work, you become more aligned, and balancing your life is that much easier. All I am really saying is that even when work has meaning, it is still not the top priority in the lives of the majority of people. Rarely will work trump family and friends.

"How many of you here today can relate to what I am talking about right now?"

Hands around the room rose up, along with knowing nods.

"How many of you would say that feeling as though you work too much and don't have enough time or energy left for family, friends, and extracurricular activities is the main reason you chose to attend this workshop today?" asked Bill.

Hands remained raised, and knowing nods continued.

"As a business owner, I have recognized and come to accept that work is not the top priority for any of my four hundred employees. I know this because I've done this workshop with my own staff many times. They've never included work as their top priority. They've never even used *one* BIG ROCK just for BILL. I'm not a priority for them, just as I can bet that no one in this workshop put me, or this workshop, down as one of their BIG ROCKS. Am I right?" asked Bill. "Did anyone save a BIG ROCK for me or this workshop? Because if you did, you get a prize.

"I'm just kidding. Trust me, I don't take it personally that you didn't include me as a priority in your lives. You can't. That is just the reality of it. Just like the fact that work is not a priority for most people. So, as a manager, the sooner you come to accept that, the easier life will be. I also think you will find it interesting that work not being a priority is not an issue that is specific to the United States. It's a common way of thinking for people across geographic boundaries. I was over in Sweden conducting this very same workshop, and I had attendees from more than sixteen European countries. The majority of them did not write down work as a top priority, just like the majority of you didn't.

"Each and every one of us needs to make a commitment to ourselves not to let our priority ROCKS get neglected, whether or not they include our careers. You will all be much better for it. Our society will be much better for it. The poet Maya Angelou once said, *I learned that making a living is not the same as making a life.'* Work is necessary, but it can't consume your lives and push it out of balance. I know that is why most of you are here. Work has caused imbalance in your lives."

"It's certainly the reason I'm here," I thought. It was nice to know I was among lots of people who were feeling my pain. People were really responding to this workshop. I was amazed at how committed my fellow workshop participants were to completing these activities. Most of the workshops I'd been to before had struggled to get to this level of participation.

This was different, though, because it hit home not only in terms of our work lives but in terms of how work intertwined or overlapped with our personal lives. What looked to be a simple exercise of identifying no more than six BIG ROCKS to label my life's true priorities had become something that was taking some careful thought when I considered it in terms of being able to manage the balance.

I needed to think things through carefully. I knew this step was crucial to the success of carrying out the rest of the activities in this workshop. Bill hadn't actually said it yet, but I saw where this discussion was leading. Bill was going to expect that I commit to the priorities I identified and had a strong belief in—a commitment to each one of my ROCKS. To think that just a few hours ago I had been handed a rock on my way into this workshop, and it had had no significance to me. Now I was thinking that this workshop might just make Pet Rocks en vogue again. I laughed to myself as my attention turned back to Bill.

EIGHT

BIG ROCKS TOOL BOX 2:

Let's Rock and Role

Now that you've identified your BIG ROCKS, you can start managing your time according to your life's true priorities. What I typically suggest at this point, when I conduct this workshop for organizations, is to get all of the employees together to share their BIG ROCKS with one another. I tend to break people into groups of no more than four to share and discuss their ROCKS. It is crucial to the process of implementing BIG ROCKS to have all employees share their priorities.

"This serves two purposes. First, it provides an opportunity for employees to get to know one another better. Second, it brings everyone together to show support for the BIG ROCKS strategy. What employees typically find is that their life's priorities don't differ so widely from those of most of their coworkers. This helps strengthen common ground between employees and allows them to begin to grow more cohesive and supportive toward one another. During this activity, I also reemphasize the concept of BIG ROCKS so employees understand why they are identifying them and what type of lifestyle this exercise will ultimately create. Also, I would like to make note of the fact that I keep talking about a lifestyle, even in the context of work. Many of you may have heard the term 'culture' as it relates to the workplace. Please note that a lifestyle is very different from a culture. Cultures are imposed upon people within an organization from the top down, whereas lifestyles are created by everyone within the organization.

"If you look again in your BIG ROCKS tool box, you will notice that the next tool available is a worksheet called ROCK AND ROLES. I would like everyone to take the identification of your BIG ROCKS one step further. I want you to now identify what role you are responsible for fulfilling for each of your BIG ROCKS. For example, if you identified one of your BIG ROCKS as your spouse, your role would be husband or wife. Next, I want you to list at least five things that you need to do to satisfy your role. For example, to satisfy my role as a husband, I make sure that I am home for dinner, that I help plan and participate in family vacations, that I take on specific household responsibilities, etc. These are just a couple of examples. My list is longer, but I think you get the idea. Again, there is a working example provided in your workbook.

"Remember that the things you do to fulfill your role are unique to you. There are no right or wrong answers. I ask only that you try to be as specific as possible. We need specific action items attached to each of your ROCKS. This will enable you to implement the strategy effectively. I'd like to say to those of you who are on the road to implementing BIG ROCKS that you need to identify at least *one* role for each ROCK and live those roles for the entire year. Are there any questions? If not, I'll give everyone ten to fifteen minutes to identify your role and the things you will do to fulfill it in relation to each of your BIG ROCKS. Please use the example to help you."

I sat and thought for a moment as I looked over the worksheet. The first thing I did was to fill in each of my BIG ROCKS on this new worksheet. I had five BIG ROCKS: Lisa, my children, family/friends, personal well-being, and career.

My role with Lisa was husband, with my children it was father, with family and friends it was friend and relative. I got a bit stuck on defining my role for my personal well-being, but ultimately I decided on facilitator because I believe that it is up to me to facilitate my own personal well-being. My role for career was financial adviser. Bill walked by, looked at what I was writing, and smiled. I asked him if I was on the right track, and he nodded and prompted me to identify the actions I would take to fulfill my roles. This was the hard part. I knew I wouldn't be able to think of everything at once.

In the role of husband to my Lisa BIG ROCK, I listed the following actions:

1. Date night: a night out for just us
2. Two weekend getaways per year
3. One annual vacation (a week to ten days)
4. One hour per day for household chores

Rock & Role

Activity Two
List Each Big Rock, Your Role & the Things to Do to Fulfill Your Role

Aligning your BIG ROCKS with your work life is vital to achieving balance in your life. Begin by identifying your role in relation to your BIG ROCKS. Next, list those tasks or things you need to do to make your BIG ROCKS a priority.

FOR EXAMPLE:

YOUR BIG ROCK	YOUR ROLE	THINGS TO DO
#1 - Wife	Husband	Out to dinner 1 night per week Gym/Sauna/Jacuzzi on Mon. & Wed. Be home for dinner Daily household chores
#2 Children	Father	Family game night Be home for dinner Help with homework Attend sports events
#3 - Health & Fitness	Athlete & Trainer	Create a personal exercise plan Run conditioning drills at co-ed training practice Join spring men's league team Pursue Personal Training License
#4 Friends/ Family	Son/Brother	Call sisters/parents once a week Send flight details to sister for spring visit Create extended family birthday planner and use it
#5 - Work	Leader	Create a time management schedule for managing new team Identify an individual educational plan for each member of the team
#6 - Personal Development	Student	Read text materials for 2 hours per day Spend alternate Saturday's completing assignments Solicit study group partners Order additional study guides

5. Share the responsibility of driving our children to their extracurricular activities
6. Family dinner on Sunday nights

In the role of father to my children BIG ROCK, I listed the following actions:

1. Attend at least 75 percent of both children's extracurricular activities
2. Provide help with homework two nights a week
3. Story time
4. One outing per month with each child—i.e., dinner, ice cream, shopping, aquarium, town/school event, etc.

In the role of friend and relative to my family and friends, I listed the following actions:

1. Three hours each week to visit with family and friends
2. Monthly dinner with the guys
3. Annual Fourth of July picnic/summer party
4. Annual Super Bowl party/winter party
5. Monthly family dinner on Sundays

In the role of facilitator for my own personal well-being, I listed the following actions:

1. One round of golf per week in season
2. Run two to three times per week (forty-five minutes each)
3. Go to the gym two to three times per week (thirty to forty-five minutes each session)
4. Read one book per month
5. Basketball with the neighborhood kids in the driveway once per week

In the role of financial adviser for my career, I listed the following actions:

1. Work no more than 8.5 hours per day
2. Take lunch and several short breaks each day

3. Reduce my number of clients by 10 percent
4. Be vocal about my needs and schedule
5. Service customers efficiently

My plans might be a little aggressive, but over the next month I'd see how they worked out and then make adjustments if I needed to. I noticed that Bill was about to ask us to wrap up this activity. I knew that I would eventually refine my list, but I thought I'd managed a good start. I hoped I had been specific enough. As I completed the worksheet, I had to say that I was beginning to feel more in control of my life than I had in some time. I was excited about all of my action ideas. They were all the things that I wanted to include in my life, and taking the time to see them written in black and white was giving me the motivation I needed to begin building them into my life. I was looking forward to finding out how to build them in. I took a second look at my action items as Bill continued with the workshop.

"I'm sure that you all have a good start on your ROCK AND ROLES worksheets. I expect that once this workshop is done, you will all revisit these worksheets. As you go about your daily lives you will, no doubt, think of other things to do or actions you would like to include in your lives. My goal today is to get you started."

"I have a question," called out a man to my left. "I have a BIG ROCK for my extended family and friends. I tend to do different things with different members of my family and friends, so it was hard for me to be specific. I just put down 'spend time' with them. Is that all right?"

Bill responded, "That's a great concept and a good start. Now I want you to expand that further to be more specific, and I'll tell you why. When we move on to the next step in this process, you will need to include these actions in your schedule—a calendar that we are going to build for you together. If you just wrote down 'spend time,' and you transfer that action item into your calendar, chances are you will probably not follow through. Write the specific name of your best friend or one of the family members that falls under this BIG ROCK."

"Umm, how about my mother? Her name is Ruth," replied the man.

"Now, if instead of writing 'spend time' you write down 'lunch with Mom every other Friday,' you will be more likely to follow through. I need everyone to be as specific as possible. The first thing you need to do if you defined your BIG ROCK as 'family and friends' is think about all of the people who fall under that ROCK. Then think about the things you typically do with them. Maybe it's a visit to their home, or maybe it's a walk, a game of golf, a lunch, or a dinner. Whatever the activity, be specific so that you increase your chances of following through," said Bill.

"I'm glad you said that," interjected a woman sitting toward the back, "because I did the same thing. One of my BIG ROCKS is fitness, and I just wrote down 'get fit.' Do you have any suggestions as to how specific I should be?"

"Well, first you need to decide how you would define 'fit' for yourself," explained Bill. "Maybe you want to lose ten pounds, maybe you want to strengthen and tone different muscle groups, maybe you want to build up your endurance. Next, you want to decide what specific activities you want to do to achieve your goal of getting fit. Maybe you want to run thirty miles per week, maybe you like tennis or swimming or roller-blading. Figure out how much time you need to dedicate to each activity you choose and then build those things into your schedule. My suggestion is to vary the activities you do each week because you will be more likely to stick with your fitness routine, but that's another workshop altogether. Understand that your list of things to do to fulfill each of your roles may be long, but it must be specific so that you can accomplish it, step by step, day by day. Does that make sense? Is everyone clear? If you weren't very specific the first time around, let's just take ten minutes to revisit your worksheets."

After ten more minutes, Bill continued, "If everyone in this room could turn and find a partner to work with, I am going to ask you to first introduce yourself to your partner if you don't already know one another and then exchange papers. Read your partner's paper and offer suggestions about their actions. As you read through the actions, if you have to ask a question about that item, then it probably could use some refining. Go ahead and get started."

I turned to the man next to me; we introduced ourselves and got right to work exchanging ideas. This was great because most of his BIG ROCKS were similar to mine. He had used a separate BIG ROCK for each of his two children, but other than that, we were in synch. Also, his action items were quite specific. Based on what I learned from him, I added a few items to my own lists. We finished up, and I was feeling quite productive and satisfied with my work so far. I was ready to move on.

Bill continued, "If it hasn't become clear to you yet, let me tell you that the reason I am asking you to be as specific as possible is because I want each one of your action items to become a goal that you alone are in control of building into your life. Remember, all goals are achieved in incremental steps. For example, your likely goal in attending this workshop was something like 'I want to change my life.' That's great, but it is too broad. Life change requires small, attainable steps or goals. This is what these action items are for you. They are the incremental goals that will lead you to achieving your ultimate goal or lifestyle change.

"What is important to point out is that when any goal is set and then met, very important things are created. They are called memories. Taking that a step further, memories that are repeated become traditions, and at the end of the day, that's what life is about.

"Does anyone here in the audience have a family tradition that is significant to them?" asked Bill.

A woman in the middle of the room spoke up and said, "Our family rents a house on the beach every year. Basically, there are three families that rent the house. The children of each family, of which I am one, all come, and we each bring a friend. Until I got married, I used to have my best girlfriend tag along. Now my husband comes, and we bring our daughter. She's the one who now brings a friend. It typically ends up being about twenty of us for ten days at the beach. We all relax and enjoy one another's company. There isn't a lot of room to sleep, but we have such a great time every year. I think we've been doing this for the last twenty-two years."

"That's a wonderful example because it spans so many years and allows me to ask you this follow-on question. Do you now recognize that when that tradition began, someone in your family had to create that experience? Someone made it a family priority to spend a vacation together and then actually planned the vacation. Obviously, it was a success because your family has continued the tradition. It is now not only a great memory for you, it is something that you look forward to each year and share with your own family. Do you recognize that someone actually created that experience?"

"I guess I never gave it much thought, especially as a teenager, but now, yes, I do recognize that it was my mother and my two aunts who initially created the experience," replied the woman in the audience.

Bill went on, "Good. Let me ask you another question, and perhaps this is a bit rhetorical, but what is it that you would like your children and/or loved ones to remember about you and their life with you? I hope you see that you can live your life by chance or you can create a lifestyle of choices and make experiences happen, just as your mother did. I personally believe that life is about choices. You may not realize it at the time that you are going through specific experiences, but after this training or workshop, I hope that perspective becomes clear to you. Too many of us believe we simply get dealt a hand and are stuck with it. The reality is that we have more choices than we realize."

NINE

BIG ROCKS TOOL BOX 3:

Lifestyle Lifelines

How often have you heard it said that if you want to achieve something, you need to start with the end in mind? Implementing the BIG ROCKS strategy is no different. Up to this point I have been taking you through activities that help you shape and identify what is important to you. This third step in the process lets you plan out on a weekly, monthly, and yearly basis how you will actually live the BIG ROCKS strategy and remain true to yourself and your life's priorities.

"The next step is completing a weekly calendar using the action items that you have defined for each of your BIG ROCKS. I have included blank calendars in your packets for you to complete today.

"The weekly calendar is the exact one we use in our organization, and it has worked well for us. Any of you that choose to download this file can feel free to modify it to meet your specific requirements. Once you complete the planner for one week, I will then move on to having you complete a monthly calendar and then a yearly calendar.

"Completing these calendars will take thought and planning on your part, so I will move everyone into groups or teams of no more than four to have you each complete your calendars. However, let's move through this process in three steps. We will all work in teams for fifteen minutes or so to complete our weekly calendars. Be sure to use the pencils I provided, as I expect many of you may be changing what you schedule within minutes after writing it. You'll be surprised at what you forgot to write in or that you may need to move an activity to another day or week. I will circulate to answer questions as you are working. I will provide examples of calendars on the screen in the front of the room as we move through each activity. Is everyone clear?"

Heads nodded in agreement, and Bill then had us break into groups of four.

"Now, before we begin to build the calendars for a week's worth of time, let me put this question out there. Can anyone tell me what the benefit is to working in teams?" asked Bill.

"Two heads are better than one," said a man in the middle of the room.

"You get different perspectives on any given issue," said another.

"Exactly right," said Bill, "And let me just add a few thoughts to that because one of the greatest benefits to working in teams is giving people the opportunity to see life through someone else's eyes. Sometimes we get so focused on ourselves that we begin to believe our way of thinking is the only way of thinking. We need to be more compassionate and understanding about where other people are coming from. It helps strengthen relationships, which is exactly what we need to do. Does anyone else want to add to our discussion and tell me more benefits to working in teams?"

"We can help each other along if anyone gets stuck," said another.

"Tasks are completed more efficiently and with greater thought and detail," said another.

"You get to hear things from your peers and hopefully build better solutions to a common problem," said someone else.

"Great," said Bill. "I think everyone is on board with the concept of working in teams. Working in teams creates a collaborative environment in which everyone feels as though they have a voice or an opportunity to contribute. Individual contribution leads to ownership, and hopefully we all recognize that if you are part of creating something, or have ownership in it, then you are more effective in implementing it.[1] Further, collaborative environments that are built on a team concept result in employees, or members within any group, making connections. Those connections lead to balance and alignment—the very reason that many of you attended today's workshop. Achieving balance and alignment results in the elimination of interference and achieving your ultimate goal of a more fulfilled life.

"Now, let me ask you a simple question that may seem like it doesn't fit with what we are talking about, but you'll just have to trust me that it does. What characteristics define a great friendship? What qualities does your best friend have?"

Audience responses began, and Bill wrote them down on white chart paper at the front of the room.

"A best friend is supportive," said one person.

"A best friend is someone that has your back, someone you can always depend on no matter what," said another.

"A best friend is someone that you can tell your secrets to, and they will keep them without judging you," said another.

"A best friend is a good listener," said another.

Bill interjected, "All right, let me ask you this. How many of you can say that you have a best friend at work?"

The room was divided fifty-fifty.

"So, why am I asking you this, and what does it have to do with balancing your lives? Well, I know that a good number of you are here because you are seeking to make your lives better by finding a way to balance your work and personal lives. You are seeking to use the BIG ROCKS strategy to achieve that. For some of you, your current working environment may adapt to, and be improved by, the changes you are implementing in your own lives. Some managers may even listen to your successes and adopt the BIG ROCKS strategy for *all* of their employees. You may be the reason your entire work lifestyle improves, not just for yourself but also for your coworkers. For many others, new jobs may be on the horizon. You may have to adapt your job to your newly created BIG ROCKS lifestyle. Therefore, I want to share a piece of research with you that you can use to analyze your current employment situation. This may be a determining factor as to whether you decide to stay or go.

"The Gallup Institute created a productive culture survey from interviewing over two million people around the world. As a result of that research, they came up with twelve factors consistent among all people in the study that were critical to their level of engagement within their organization. One of the key factors for heightening engagement was having a best friend at work. Now, many of you may be perplexed about the notion of having a best friend at work because we've grown up in a world where spending time with people during work hours was considered idle time or unproductive time. Thus, there was no time for building friendships in the workplace. We now know that just the opposite is true. In order to get the most productivity from people and sustain solid retention rates, we need to ensure that people connect meaning to their work. Genuine connections between people give meaning to work.

"I talked to you earlier about engagement. The Gallup Organization was the first to define this term as it relates to the workplace. Previous to its labeling this concept, we didn't have a specific, focused terminology to explain positive and productive behaviors—those things that are working and that people do well. On the other hand, we have plenty of terms to describe episodes of behavior that occur when people are not well, things that ail the human mind. If I mentioned the terms 'schizophrenia,' 'bipolarism,' 'disassociative or hyperactivity disorders,' 'psychosis,' 'neurosis,' etc. you would all know the types of behaviors I am speaking about because we have a language for them. In psychological terms we have an entire volume of information called the DSM IV [*Diagnostic and Statistical Manual for Mental Disorders,* fourth edition] to describe behaviors that occur when people's minds are not well. The goal for practitioners was to bring people from this 'not well' state back to a neutral normal state. Up until recent times, the goal of the practitioner has been to stamp out disabling conditions. As a collective society, we have spent the last half-century labeling the things that are 'not right' with people in our society. We have very clear terms for these things. Aside from the technical terms I just mentioned, everyday negative language is used all too often. Has anyone here ever been called a 'know-it-all,' 'bossy,' 'picky,' 'snobby,' a 'chatterbox'? Those are all pretty negative terms that are used often. Would you agree? Does everyone recognize the terms I've just mentioned? Collectively, our goal, moving into the future, must be to turn the negative language around and highlight the positive aspects of those traits that are currently perceived as negative."

Heads throughout the audience bobbed up and down with an emphatic "yes."

"Here's another question to further clarify this point. Has anyone here ever had a performance review at their job?" Just about everyone nodded in agreement. "Did you ever stop to analyze how much time was spent on what you were doing well versus how much time was spent on the areas in which you needed improvement? If you did analyze it, you might find that the majority of the time was spent on your weaknesses.[2]

"Now, as it relates to describing positive behaviors or the things that people do well, the best we've been able to do is explain it on a superficial level. If I asked you to give me a term for people who have a relationship that works, what academic term or expression would you give me?"

Everyone looked around the room, waiting for someone else to respond;

the silence grew … finally, Bill jumped back in and said, "The reason you cannot think of any academic term is because there aren't any that you are familiar with. I've introduced you to the Gallup term, 'engagement,' and the Focus Group term, 'alignment,' but my guess is that those are new terms to you for explaining positive interactive relationships. Can anyone give me a common everyday expression that you would use to describe two people who are in a relationship that works?"

Again there was a short pause before a woman in the middle of the room spoke. "I would say that they 'get along well' or they 'jell.'"

"Good. Anyone else have another expression?

"How about that they 'mesh'?"

"Good. Anything else?"

"How about saying that they 'hit it off'?"

"Anything else?" Bill waited a short moment before saying, "How about what we typically say in relation to sports teams, that they have 'great chemistry'? That's probably the best we've come up with to describe it. In our society, we are lacking positive terms. It makes you wonder why there always seems to be so much negativity. It's time for us to study and identify the conditions that allow human beings to thrive. There is currently a groundswell of research emerging to look at 'the sunny side' of human behavior.

"When people feel connected and valued, they become more committed to any organization or team. Once they are committed, they work hard for the organization because they want to benefit not just themselves but everyone they work with. Having a best friend at work or cultivating great friendships in the work environment elevates a person's level of engagement, which ultimately leads to increased productivity and corporate profit.[3] Now, some of you may be feeling that the concept of having a best friend at work is foreign to you. You may be thinking you don't have a best friend at work because you hold the image of your spouse or the friend you've had since grammar school in your head when you think 'best friend.' You know, the person with whom you share all of your personal triumphs and tragedies. The 'best friend' at work doesn't have to be that intense. What the research is saying is that people who have sought out and identified a 'best friend' at work have found a person whom they work with who has all of the qualities that they would look for in a best friend.

"Now, let's move on with your weekly calendars. Please note that your calendars may change after you leave here today and think of more items to add. I want to walk you through the exercise so you have the tools and the practical knowledge you need to maintain up-to-date calendars. What I don't want you to do is complete these calendars today and then never look at them again. Ultimately, they should become your lifestyle lifeline to implementing change using the BIG ROCKS strategy. I am putting the ball in your court. It's about taking responsibility for how successful you are in making improvements from this day forward. I will warn you that it is not easy. It requires a daily commitment. At the start of each new day, you must renew your commitment to living the BIG ROCKS strategy.

"As an employee, one of your greatest time-management BIG ROCKS tools will be your weekly calendar. This calendar will allow you to time both your personal and professional lives in a way that makes your life easier to manage. The difference between this calendar and a typical time-management schedule, however, is that you are ensuring that your BIG ROCKS are listed.

"It may sound as if I am creating a lot of work for you right now, but as you move through these calendars you will see how much overlap there is between them. Eventually, the calendars will all fit together to complete the puzzle of your individual lives.

"So, to begin, take the next fifteen minutes or so to fill in the weekly calendar. Use the action items from your ROCK AND ROLES worksheet. You may have some action items that don't belong in your weekly calendar. Save those for the monthly or yearly calendars. Eventually, everything will come together.

"When completing your weekly calendar, I want to make sure that everyone is clear that it is not just for work-related tasks. Your life is much more than just your job. Use the calendar as your guide to understanding just how full your life is and how it is possible to make time for all of the things that are important to you. This calendar is also for your personal and social commitments. You need to put everything on the same calendar. Once you can see it in black and white, trust me, it will really help you not only to manage your time but to keep your life's true priorities in balance."

Bill walked over to get a cup of coffee as the rest of us got busy completing our calendars. I worked hard to complete the weekly planning pages, and I was amazed at how quickly I filled everything in. Also, it was very helpful to see everything laid out in front of me to balance the time.

WORKING EXAMPLE OF WEEKLY CALENDARS

WEEKLY SCHEDULE

Name:

For the Week Beginning:

A.M.	SUN	MON	TUE	WED	THU	FRI	SAT
5	Sleep	Sleep	Sleep	Sleep	Sleep	Sleep	Sleep
:30	Sleep	Sleep	Sleep	Sleep	Sleep	Sleep	Sleep
6	Sleep	Sleep	Sleep	Sleep	Sleep	Wake, Coffee & Shower	Sleep
:30	Sleep	Wake, Coffee & Shower	Wake, Coffee & Shower	Wake, Coffee & Shower	Wake, Coffee & Shower	Check E-Mail	Sleep
7	Sleep	Check E-Mail	Check E-Mail	Check E-Mail	Check E-Mail	Call Dave J	Wake, Coffee & Shower
:30	Wake, Coffee & Shower	Miscellaneous ELT Projects	Call Jamie M			Call Dave J/ Call Roy C	Travel
8	Soccer TV	Miscellaneous ELT Projects	Call Adi M		Sporting Essentials Call	Call Roy C	University Class
:30	Soccer TV	Miscellaneous ELT Projects	Call James H		Sporting Essentials Call	Call Deven A	University Class
9	Soccer TV	Miscellaneous ELT Projects	Call Paul M.	Marketing Call		Call Deven A/ Call Gary O	University Class
:30	Travel	Miscellaneous ELT Projects	Prep Call	Marketing Call		Call Gary O	University Class
10	Soccer Practice	Check E-Mail	Conference Call	Marketing Call		Call Brett R	University Class
:30	Soccer Practice	Return Calls	Conference Call	Marketing Call Notes		Call Brett R/ Call Dave A	University Class
11	Soccer Practice		Call Barry M			Call Dave A	University Class

WORKING EXAMPLE OF WEEKLY CALENDARS

	SUN	MON	TUE	WED	THU	FRI	SAT
:30	Soccer Practice		Call Neil D			Call Adam G	University Class
P.M. 12	Travel		Return E-Mail			Call Adam G/ Call Justin H	Lunch
:30	Rest		Lunch Break			Call Justin H	Lunch
1	Rest		Call Sean C			Call Justin H/ Call Scott R	University Class
:30	Rest		Call Spencer H			Call Scott R	University Class
2	Bike Ride	Review Marketing Projects	Contract Re-Write			Call Mark H	University Class
:30	Bike Ride		Contract Re-Write			Call Mark H/ Call Neil D	University Class
3	Online	Complete BIG ROCKS document	Outbound E-Mail Correspondence			Call Neil D	University Class
:30	Online	Complete BIG ROCKS document	Travel		Travel	CRM Report Summary	University Class
4	Sauna & Jacuzzi	MBA Study Time	Soccer Practice	MBA Study Time	Soccer Practice	CRM Report Summary	University Class
:30	Sauna & Jacuzzi	MBA Study Time	Soccer Practice	MBA Study Time	Soccer Practice	Follow Up E-Mail Correspondence	University Class
5	Shower	MBA Study Time	Soccer Practice	MBA Study Time	Soccer Practice	Gym	Travel
:30	Travel	MBA Study Time	Travel	MBA Study Time	Travel	Gym	Rest

WORKING EXAMPLE OF WEEKLY CALENDARS

P.M.	SUN	MON	TUE	WED	THU	FRI	SAT
6	Dinner with Friends	Gym	Return Calls	Gym	Return Calls	Sauna & Jacuzzi	Sauna & Jacuzzi
:30	Dinner with Friends	Gym	E-Mail Correspondence	Gym	E-Mail Correspondence	Prepare Dinner	Sauna & Jacuzzi
7	Dinner with Friends	Sauna & Jacuzzi	Sauna & Jacuzzi	Sauna & Jacuzzi	Sauna & Jacuzzi	Dinner with wife	Dinner with Friends
:30	Dinner with Friends	Prepare Dinner	Sauna & Jacuzzi	Prepare Dinner	Sauna & Jacuzzi	Board Games	Dinner with Friends
8	Dinner with Friends	Dinner with wife	Prepare Dinner	Dinner with wife	Prepare Dinner	Board Games	Dinner with Friends
:30	Dinner with Friends	Check E-Mail	Dinner with wife	Check E-Mail	Dinner with wife	TV Time	Dinner with Friends
9	Dinner with Friends	MBA Online Research	TV Time	MBA Online Friends	Personal Reading	TV Time	Coffee
:30	Dinner with Friends	MBA Online Research	TV Time	MBA Online Friends	Personal Reading	TV Time	Walk
10	Travel	Bed	Bed	Bed	Bed	Bed	Bed
:30	Bed	Bed	Bed	Bed	Bed	Bed	Bed
11	Sleep	Sleep	Sleep	Sleep	Sleep	Sleep	Sleep
:30	Sleep	Sleep	Sleep	Sleep	Sleep	Sleep	Sleep

"Has everyone completed their pages?" Bill asked after about fifteen minutes.

Most of the heads around the room nodded, but one hand, belonging to a man to my left, was raised. "Could I have just a few more minutes?" he asked. "I thought I was done, but when I went back over my calendar I realized that I had left out several items that I wanted to put in. Sorry, I'll just be a minute."

"Take your time; that's quite all right. In fact, it is normal for that to happen. We all have good intentions about fitting everything in, but it is difficult to do. Using these calendars forces you to be realistic about what you do in fact have time for. What are you going to do to fix it?"

"Well, I'm just erasing some things right now and moving them around. You were right when you said that this was going to be like a puzzle because that is exactly what I feel like I'm building."

"Go ahead and fit in the items you need. While you are taking a few more minutes to finish, I suggest that everyone else take the time to double-check that all of the items from their ROCK AND ROLES sheets have been accounted for on the weekly calendar," said Bill.

"If you were to have everyone in your organization create one of these weekly calendars, you would need to check to make sure they were diligent about maintaining them so they were able to balance their time. Oftentimes with my employees, I may look at a calendar and notice that they are not spending enough time at home or with their family because they are putting in too many hours at work. I will talk to them about it and encourage them to change their schedule. That may sound like a novel idea, and you may be wondering why I wouldn't want to get more time out of my employees. The reason is that it is just time, and if they are tired and/or burned out, how much productive time are they really giving me, and how valued do you think they feel?

"Employees who are overworked feel devalued and detached from their jobs. They feel isolated and are more likely to leave an organization or stop caring about their work. Further, I don't believe that crunching more hours out of people is ethical. If you are managing a group of people and you say that you genuinely care about those people and you are creating a 'people-centric' environment, then why would you even think about overusing those people? Doing so will ultimately lead to disengaged employees, lower retention rates, and weakened productivity.

"In fact, the greatest issues facing any organization that must be dealt with to ensure business survival are retention, productivity, and performance. I believe that individuals, teams, and organizations must focus on people as the answer to the growth and development of our world's alignment and every facet within it. People must be given the opportunity to be involved in more decision-making. They must be afforded more autonomy and ownership in their work.

"Past philosophies believed that people needed to be watched and told what to do because they were incapable of making good choices. The reality is that no one likes to be watched or told what to do, and most people can be trusted to make good choices. Therefore, businesses need to adopt a systematic approach for leading their people to effectively fulfill their roles—*a people system.*

"A people system must meet the needs of all of the people in it. As you all know, meeting the needs of everyone within an organization is not an easy thing to do. It's something that requires constant attention because people's needs vary widely and change over time. We are all different. We may have different values, beliefs, and cultural backgrounds. We certainly all have different life experiences. All of these differences shape us and make us unique human beings. It is important to remember this simple fact as you think about your colleagues at work and your family at home. We all have intolerant attitudes toward the behavior of others. We all have our pet peeves. However, it is how we manage those attitudes that measures the strength of our character. We can either accept, and even embrace, differences or let our intolerance control us. If you choose to let intolerance control you, I can tell you that it is a huge waste of your valuable energy. Why spend time being upset over what you cannot change in someone else? Wouldn't that energy be much better focused on your own growth and change?

"By nature, I have always been driven to find out how and why things work. So when I identified the correlation between meeting my employees' needs and the success of my business, I wanted to capture those intangible steps. I now refer to the intangible steps that work to enable and engage employees as 'people processes.'[4] If you stop and think about it, all businesses have processes for their day-to-day functions. Can anyone give me an example?"

A man in the back of the room called out, "Are you talking about things like accounting processes or marketing and communications processes?"

"Exactly," said Bill. "Those are good examples. Now, with those in mind, you should have a better understanding of what I was trying to do with my own company and what I have worked to create. I wanted to develop a concrete, repeatable process that works to strengthen communication and human interaction. I wanted the process to activate individuals toward autonomy; build trusting, caring, and respectful relationships; and develop a sense of pride and ownership in professional responsibilities within each individual and groups of individuals within my organization. I wanted to understand the actual steps involved in creating successful people processes.

"In the past, we emphasized the development of physical systems for the effective fulfillment of roles. Generally Accepted Accounting Principles (GAAPs) were developed for finance, Standard Operating Procedures (SOPs) for operations, and technical procedures for information technology. Companies have grown by leaps and bounds with these dependable systems in place, yet most aren't maximizing the potential of their human capital. Human capital, or a company's employees, should be managed with the same detail and diligence as an organization's finance department. Together, these are the two departments that should be driving any company. As Jack Welch, former CEO of General Electric put it, *'Any company trying to compete ... must figure out a way to engage the mind of nearly every employee.'*

"When I first read that quote, I thought it was great that we have high-level leaders who recognize this key component to business success. My next thought was, 'So why aren't there people systems in place to ensure that this happens?'" said Bill. "Ask any supervisor in an organization, 'Do you have to deal with more issues with physical systems or people?' The answer is always 'People,' and that's why creating or adopting a system to lead the people within any organization is so vital. Isn't it ironic that most companies hire people to monitor their IT [information technology] systems on a daily basis, yet those same organizations put hundreds of thousands of people together on a daily basis and simply expect it to work with no monitoring or management in place?

"Organizations have experienced the Industrial and Technology Ages, but it's my candid belief that today is, without a doubt, the **People Age**.[5] As former Citibank CEO Dee Hook put it, *'Whoever is the first to harness the collective genius of his or her workforce will blow the competition away.'* So let me ask you, as individuals, are you interested in finding meaningful employment that sustains you over the long term? Are you interested in working for an organization where you feel valued and involved? Do you want to be trusted with key decisions in your role?

"Let me ask you as organizational leaders, are you interested in reducing attrition, retaining key staff and clients, developing talent—'blowing the competition away'? If so, then you must consider adopting new philosophies and methods of leading your people. You must find out what is *important* to your employees. You must help them balance their lives, and the BIG ROCKS strategy is one of the key components to helping you achieve success first for yourselves, then for your employees. It's not about getting more hours from your employees; it's about getting a higher number of *productive hours.* To do that, those employees must have balanced lives. As a manager, you must recognize that people's personal and professional lives are intertwined, and their personal lives are extremely important to their consistently delivering productive working hours.

"As I said before when you defined your BIG ROCKS, family, friends, and free time are what reenergize us. They are the source of our strength and greatest joy. If my employees are reenergized, I get more productive time out of them. And that is the key. I told you that managing the BIG ROCKS strategy takes continuous effort. The rewards, however, are great. Consider that the turnover rate in my organization is less than 3 percent per year. Consider that absenteeism is even less than that. This is significant because absenteeism—all forms such as injury, illness, turnover, and fraud—is a billion-dollar problem every year in this country. Across the world it is a trillion-dollar problem.[6]

"One of the greatest contributors to my own business success is that I'm a firm believer in the notion that people need to plan their vacation time, and they need to take it.[7] In fact, in my company our fiscal year begins in January, and that is when my employees build their yearly calendars. Vacations and holiday time are the first thing I ask them to plan for, and when you really think about it, this is one of my corporation's BIG ROCKS. I can attest to the fact that this belief enhances productivity. In fact, because my employees are engaged and I have strong internal retention, that translates into my client retention rate being 87 to 91 percent every year.

"I know that there are many companies out there that measure success by the number of hours and days each of their employees works. They believe that they are increasing productivity. I'm proud to say that we are not one of those companies. Based on my experience, I find that it's vital to ensure that employees have enough holiday time. As a leader, there is a responsibility to play an active part in helping employees achieve balance. If you are an effective leader, you already know the value in serving your employees. Leadership is about serving your employees. It is not about them serving you.

"Now, some of you may be thinking that there are employees who will abuse this type of environment. Yes, you're right, there are those who will take advantage of this system, but in my experience those employees are few and far between once they have had an opportunity to create their company lifestyle. Again, involve people and you will be amazed at the results! However, if you find these people working in your organization, the responsibility falls on hiring practices. Companies must be diligent in finding employees who honestly subscribe to your company's lifestyle. They must seek out employees who are a match for different roles and responsibilities. In the book *Good to Great*, Jim Collins found through his research that 'great' companies never settle. If they are hiring for a specific position, they don't just hire someone with 75 percent of the skills because they have a need to fill a job. They are patient, and they wait for just the right individual.

"For anyone interested in learning more about effectively leading employees and ensuring that each employee is fulfilling the right role within the company, I would recommend Jim Collins's book *Good to Great*. Essentially, what Collins's research shows is that in order to take a company from good to great, you have to answer the question 'Who?' (Do you have the right people in your company, those who subscribe to the core values of the company?) before you can define 'What?' (What's the strategy or direction the company is choosing to follow?). Collins's research shows that it is only after you have all of the right people in the organization that you can decide on the direction in which those people are going to drive the company. Collins uses the metaphor of a bus and asserts that in order to drive the bus (the company) to greatness, all the right employees must not only be on the bus but must also be in the right seats. (People must be put into the right roles and given responsibilities based on their talents.)

"Research from the Gallup Organization, although conducted independently, supports this idea. Gallup says that in order to put all of the people within an organization in the right seats, you must conduct employee talent profiles. Conducting talent profiles and fitting the right people together in a work environment ties in with the whole idea of lifestyle. This in turn ties into the Focus Group processes of balance and alignment. Now, enough explanations; let me check in on everyone's progress on their weekly calendars. Is everyone finished?" asked Bill.

Everyone had completed his or her calendar.

"Let's move on to completing our monthly calendars. I would like you to work in your groups. Use your weekly calendars to put your action items into the amount of monthly hours you'll spend on them. Be sure to include your personal engagements to balance your priorities. The monthly calendar gives you a different view of your time because you are looking at a thirty-day picture. Some of you may find this to be the most challenging calendar to complete. Feel free to use the example on the screen to help you. As you work, I will circulate to answer questions. Go ahead and begin."

We all began filling in our monthly calendars. Working in groups allowed us to be more productive because we could help each other along if any questions arose.

My group finished our monthly calendars before a lot of the others, so I had an opportunity to look around and listen in on the interaction that was going on in other groups. This was exactly what Bill was talking about when he mentioned the benefit of working in teams. This strategy was certainly keeping people on task and engaged.

Everyone continued, and the monthly calendars went very smoothly. Next we moved on to completing our yearly calendars to get the "big-picture" view of our lives. This was the calendar on which all the major events of both our personal and professional lives got mapped out. Bill showed us examples on the screen, and by the time we finished I thought everyone was in agreement that we had a very good start toward living the BIG ROCKS strategy.

"Before we finish our calendars, I have a question," said a workshop participant. "Wouldn't it have been easier to start with the big-picture view, or the yearly calendar, and then work our way back?"

"Good observation," replied Bill. "The next time you plan out a year, that is exactly what you will do. You will start with the yearly calendar and then move to the monthly and then to the weekly. I did it this way on purpose. I wanted you to identify your priorities and then fit them in. Doing the calen-

MONTHLY CALENDAR

Now fill out your own monthly calender ... don't forget your BIG ROCKS!

Name		Department	Exec. VP
Month	January	Days Available for Month	31
Hours Each Day	24	Total Hrs. Available for Month	744
		Total Hrs. Left for Month	

Categories for the Month	
Sleep	Work
Significant Other	Sport
Exercise	Family
School	

Monthly Breakdown by Category	Hrs.	Priority
Sleep	248	2
Work Tasks	238	3
Baltimore National Training	60	
Calls/Contact with Development Coordinators	48	
Document Review Time	10	
Proposals	10	
Contracts/Tasks	8	
Reorganization of VP Responsibilities	6	
Contract Negotiation with XYZ Corp	2	
Creation/Editing of Tracking & Reporting Documents	20	
Marketing Meetings and Proofs	8	
SE Meetings, Review Time and Projects	8	
ELT Prep and Meetings	12	
Education & Training Lesson Plans and Handouts	6	
Significant Other	56	1
Prepare Dinner and Eat Together	24	
Exercise Together	8	
Dinner with Friends	12	
TV Time	8	
Board Games	4	
Sport	52	5
Tues/Thurs/Sunday Practice Sessions	24	
Golf	4	
Snowboarding Trip	24	
Exercise	19	6
Create Exercise Plan	2	
Gym, Sauna, Jacuzzi (M, TH, FR, SUN)	16	
Complete NPTI Application Forms	1	
Family	10	7
Weekly Call to Parents/Sister	8	
E-Mail Correspondence	2	
School	88	4
Class	32	
Readings	28	
Study Groups	8	
Assignments	20	
Unassigned	33	8
TOTAL HOURS		

YEARLY SCHEDULE FORM

Now plan your own yearly schedule, and be sure to include your BIG ROCKS wherever you can!

JANUARY	FEBRUARY	MARCH
Book vacations and business trips Weekend in Tahoe Complete Tax Returns Manage investments	Group Class assignments Buy a new car	Class assignments Commence spring men's and co-ed soccer season
APRIL	**MAY**	**JUNE**
Ski vacation in Tahoe Trip to Georgia to play Sugar Loaf & attend the Masters Travel to UK - convention	Get ahead on reading for summer MBA semester Begin personal training course	Take rock climbing class in preparation for Tahoe trip
JULY	**AUGUST**	**SEPTEMBER**
Camping/climbing vacation in Tahoe	Begin to get ahead on reading for fall semester Annual pilgrimage to Oneonta Birthday celebration	Begin house hunting Vacation in Hawaii Begin fall MBA classes
OCTOBER	**NOVEMBER**	**DECEMBER**
Purchase a home	Thanksgiving Birthday celebration - wife	Yearly planning Christmas holiday

dars this way the first time helps you 'build up' to the big picture of your life. Now that you have the big picture in the forefront of your mind, you can tackle your calendars from the opposite direction. Any other questions?

"Great; you have just completed the three basic steps to beginning your journey toward actively living BIG ROCKS. You've

1. Identified your BIG ROCKS (life's true priorities),
2. Tied roles and action items to your BIG ROCKS, and
3. Built your priorities into weekly, monthly, and yearly calendars.

"Now that everything is spelled out for you in black and white, it's time for the real work to begin. Now you have to live it."

TEN

BIG ROCKS TOOL BOX 4:

Actively Living
BIG ROCKS

ill went on, "Now that your BIG ROCKS have been identified and your calendars are complete, I would like to share with you how to actively live the BIG ROCKS strategy.

"When you leave here today, you need to take the time to review your calendars and make any necessary revisions. What I typically suggest to anyone new to living the BIG ROCKS strategy is that you rely heavily on your weekly calendars for the first four weeks to see if what you've planned is realistic. If you are still struggling, change some things around and reorganize your time until it works for you.

"Once your calendar is as complete as possible, begin to apply the principles I am going to share with you now to actively live the BIG ROCKS strategy. At first, the principles for actively living BIG ROCKS sound very simple: planning your time in accordance with your BIG ROCKS and eliminating interference. However, implementing them will require daily effort from you. Eventually, though, these principles should become second nature—where you don't even think about them anymore, you just live them.

"You have already begun to apply the FIRST PRINCIPLE, which is **Plan Your Time from the Big-Picture Perspective.** You have created detailed calendars that include daily action items that move you toward your goal of making meaningful changes in your life. You continue this effort by filling details into your calendars as they become available. Try to look at least a month ahead.

"The SECOND PRINCIPLE revolves around **Removing the Interference in**

Your Life. The first step is to recognize and identify the interference in your life, and the second step is to eliminate it. Now, this doesn't mean that you no longer allow some interference in your life, because there are unplanned events or opportunities that come along that you may welcome. If you reflect back on the activity I did with the bowl, I think you would agree that there was room for some sand, pebbles, and even water—but you need to know when to say when. The idea is to not let interference push your big rocks right out of the bowl. The key is to adopt a better strategy for managing the interference by being choosy about what you accept into your calendar.

"This is not to say you should push spontaneity out of your lives. You should leave enough room to take advantage of spontaneous opportunities as they come along.

"Remember earlier when I told you it was up to you to determine how full your bowls are according to your own definition of full? For some of you, a full bowl may be only your rocks and some pebbles; for others it may be your rocks, some pebbles, sand, and even a little water. You choose your own level of full. My recommendation would be to always leave room in your proverbial bowls. If you think back to the activity, everyone should have agreed that the bowl was as full as it could be when there was still enough room for another full glass of water. The point is that there always needs to be space for something extra ... something unexpected.

"Seeing your weekly activities on paper in front of you provides a visual representation of how you are spending your time. You will quickly realize how little time you may have for yourself. Those of you who are technically savvy could build graphics into your calendar to graph how much time you actually contribute to each of your BIG ROCKS. To do this you would have to categorize your time and perhaps use an Excel spreadsheet to create some interesting graphs. This will be useful for those of you who are visual learners. It is not unlike the graphs credit-card companies include when they send you an account summary at the end of each year to tell you how much money you spent on food, clothing, travel, car expenses, entertainment, etc. Is everyone familiar with these types of account summaries?" asked Bill.

Many attendees raised their hands.

"Well, this is a similar idea," explained Bill, "and again, I understand that for some of you it may be completely over the top. However, there are those who may find it easy and very helpful. Whether you prefer to create your calendars electronically or simply by using paper and pencil, the real value of the calendars centers on reflection. Your calendars will be your window into seeing just how much you accomplished in a given week, month, and year. They will also give you a place to write down both your personal and your professional goals and help keep you true to those goals. Writing it down helps you to commit to it and focus on it.

"Now, let's look at eliminating interference. How do you do that? Well, first let's revisit our definition of interference. *Interference is the difference between where you want to be and where you believe you are. It is really whatever in your life is blocking you from nurturing your true priorities.* So, for example, if you have plans for a dinner out with your significant other, and your boss asks you to work late at the last minute, that would be considered interference that likely should be eliminated. Or maybe you have plans several months from now to take some vacation time, and let's suppose that you plan to not go anywhere but simply stay home and relax. However, a family member asks if you can help them with a major home improvement project because they know you have that time off. That would be considered interference. This second example is a difficult one. Most of us are so used to keeping busy that we feel guilty about taking time off to simply relax. Instead we fill our relaxation time with things to do that we may not really feel like doing. Then we complain and feel even more stressed and irritated. How many people in this room can relate to the picture I am painting right now?" asked Bill.

I think every hand in the room went up, including mine.

"Of course you do," said Bill emphatically. "You wouldn't be here if you didn't relate to that simple fact. Therefore, I'm telling you to go with the relaxation and learn to stop feeling guilty. Now more than ever, we all need down time. Just like we all need to eat, drink enough water, exercise, and get enough sleep to stay healthy, we all need relaxation time. It keeps our minds healthy. I promise you that you will feel more fulfilled, be more productive, and just come across as more pleasant to be around if you take time for yourself.

"What are some of the ways you enjoy relaxing? For me it's spending time with family, traveling, reading a good book, maybe going out for a meal or going to the beach. Sometimes it is simply doing nothing at all. I want you to take a few minutes right now to write down the relaxation activities that are most appealing to you."

On the back of my ROCK AND ROLES worksheet I wrote the following list:

Ways to Relax

- Reading the newspaper
- Watching sports with Jake
- Watching movies at home on the couch
- Taking the family out for dinner
- Walking on the beach
- Dinner out with members of my extended family
- Using the hot tub
- Soccer and baseball games out on the lawn with the kids and their friends
- Watching a major sporting event at home with my friends

"Is everyone finished?" asked Bill as he looked around the room to find that all of us were done. I thought that this had been the easiest activity for me so far.

Bill continued, "Great! Now that you are done I want you to double-check to see that these things are in your calendars. I plan my relaxation time or down time at exactly the same time each week. Because of this, my relaxation time has become a habit for me. This may be a strategy that will work for you, too. Also, I have certain action items on my calendar that are non-negotiable. For example, I make it a point to be home for dinner every night, no matter what, unless of course I am traveling. That time for me is non-negotiable, and it is something my family can always depend on.

"A critical step toward eliminating interference is learning to say no. In my experience, I find this to be especially difficult for women. Now, I realize that is not true for all women and I'm making a generalization here, but I believe it's an accurate one. Too often, women seem to be asked, or choose, to be all things to all people in their lives, and that can be a big burden—especially for women not skilled at saying no. Yet once you learn to say no, your life will run a whole lot more smoothly, your stress level will decrease, and your outlook will be more positive.

"Additionally, you will become more productive at the things you do include in your schedule. Most of us try to pack too many things into our weekly schedules, and then we feel stressed about failing to complete all of them. Therefore, I'm suggesting that you build fewer things into your weekly calendar. This will give you a better chance at completing all of the things that you want to so that you feel productive. To make this happen, you must learn to say no and eliminate the interference in your life.

"Don't be alarmed if you upset some people along the way by saying no. Deal with it and recognize that it's their problem, and if they truly have respect for you, then they'll get over it. Also, if you say no to the things you really can't do, or don't want to do, often enough, people will eventually stop asking. This will make eliminating interference that much easier for you.

"The way I see it, you have a choice. You can either let the interference that other people create in your life control you, or you can control it. I understand that most of us have a need to please the people around us, and we want to help whenever we can. That's great and admirable. However, when it results in widening the gap between what you say you want and what you actually have, then you must learn to eliminate it or you will forever feel overwhelmed. This will only serve to send you right back to conferences like this. Not that I wouldn't want to see you again, but my goal in conducting this workshop is to get you to a point where I'm no longer needed.

"The whole idea behind doing a calendar focuses you on mapping out your time. For most of us, seeing it in black and white on paper in front of us accomplishes two goals. First, it lets us see how busy we really are, and second, it ensures that we make priority time for the BIG ROCKS in our lives. Remember, earlier I told you that I make my staff put in their vacations first at the beginning of the year. I tell them to also plan for birthdays and holidays or other significant events. If they have a circle of friends who are important to them and have been identified as one of their BIG ROCKS, I might say, plan a night out or a dinner and call all of those friends so that the event is on their calendars, too. Then I make sure they complete their calendars, looking one month ahead at a minimum. If they can look ahead further with significant details, that's even better.

"I am diligent about making sure that the people who have been on my staff for five years or less focus on completing calendars. These are employees who typically need to create the habit of prioritizing their BIG ROCKS because for most of them, it's a totally new concept in their lives. I check over their calendars and make suggestions to help them maintain the balance in their lives.

"Equally, I have staff who have been with me for many years and have become so familiar with living the BIG ROCKS strategy that they don't even really need their calendars. The BIG ROCKS strategy has become a way of life, a habit or a lifestyle for them. They may use a calendar to plan for major events such as vacations, holidays, and business trips and have a fair amount of detail. However, I am not as strict with my longer-term employees because they have proven their commitment to actively living the BIG ROCKS strategy.

"If you follow this strategy, then eventually that is where you will end up. Some of you may decide to keep doing the calendars because it will be a helpful habit by then. Others may modify or eliminate the calendar. I still use my calendars, and I've been doing this for a long time. I find that the calendars help me feel organized, especially when life begins to become overwhelming. Revisiting my calendar and viewing my time in an organized fashion helps bring me back into focus or back into balance."

As he paused, a man sitting two rows over from me responded, "Completing the calendars seems like an awful lot of work to me. I'm not sure I would be able to be diligent about sticking to it after the first several weeks or the first month or so."

"I'm glad you voiced that concern," answered Bill. "It is one that others, no doubt, have as well. Often, workshop participants say, 'I don't have enough time for time management,' and I think that's what you're feeling based on your question."

The man nodded in agreement.

"But remember, you are here because you want to make meaningful changes in your life, and that requires you to take responsibility and put forth some effort. My suggestion would be to carve out a chunk of time to do the initial setup of your first calendar. In fact, you have a great framework already because of the work we've done together today. All you need to do is build in fifteen to thirty minutes each day. Maybe it will be first thing in the morning or late in the evening. Whatever works for you. Once you get the initial calendar complete, updating it will become easier from month to month and from year to year.

"Remember, this is a lifestyle change. If it is truly important to you— which I think it is based on the fact that you came to this workshop—you will find the time to get it done. Remember, as I told you before, that life is about choices. Keep in mind that you made the choice to come here today to learn how to balance your life. I hope you will also make the choice to give this a chance and follow through with it.

"The calendar is, in a sense, your crutch until you are able to fly with this strategy on your own. It is vital that you begin the implementation by creating your calendars. They are your lifestyle lifelines. If you were in financial trouble and you hired a planner, the first thing they would have you do is write down all of your expenses and all of your income in order to come up with a plan that works for your individual life. Writing it all out would help you and a financial planner understand the issues, deliver a solution, and then measure progress. As it relates to the BIG ROCKS strategy, creating the calendars helps measure your progress. It's the only way you are going to begin to actively live BIG ROCKS," explained Bill as he pointed to another workshop participant who had a question. "Yes, Miss, what's your question?"

"You mentioned that it is particularly difficult for women to learn to say no to interference. I completely agree with that because I am one of those women!" stated a dark-haired woman in the back of the room. "Do you have any advice and suggestions as to how to learn to be comfortable saying no?"

"Great question," enthused Bill. "The first thing I will tell you to do once your initial calendars are complete is to say no to everything you haven't planned for. You need to find a way to eliminate the pressure that comes with being put on the spot and get people to back off. When anyone is put on the spot and caught off guard by interference, they will say yes quickly more often than not. Change that behavior by first asking a clarifying question such as 'Why do you ask?' in order to understand the reason behind the request. Then, depending on what they have asked you to do, you can give a flat-out no or a maybe. This is your replacement behavior. Anytime you would be inclined to say yes, say maybe or say no instead. I will even give you my top phrases for saying no or maybe. You're welcome to use them or change them to suit your personality. Either way, I would suggest memorizing a few of them. This way, when someone puts you on the spot, you are ready with a response. Practice saying them out loud to yourself ... perhaps while you are driving. You may say something such as:

1. I'm sorry. I wish I could help, but I'm not available (this evening, that day, at that time, etc.).
2. My calendar is quite full right now, so I'm not sure I can make it.

Let me know what you specifically need, and I'll check my calendar and get back to you.

3. I already have a previous commitment. If I'd had more notice I might have been able to help you out.
4. It really isn't a good time. I have a lot going on at home right now.
5. I can do that for you, but I also have (X, Y, and Z) on my plate, and I need to check the priority of what needs to get done.
6. I'm not saying yes, but if I could do X, I will need to think about it first and get back to you.

"I would suggest being as concise as possible. Don't feel that you have to give an elaborate excuse as to why you are unavailable. Remember, they are asking you for your time. If you say it's not available, that means that it is not available. Try to avoid making excuses. Some people tend to try to think of elaborate excuses to avoid hurting others' feelings. Like I said earlier, you may upset people along the way, but they need to learn to respect your boundaries, and you need to learn how to set them.

"Before we wrap up this workshop session today, I would like you to flip through your workbook materials and review several things. First, I would like you to review the answers to the questions I posed to you in the beginning of this presentation: **Write down JUST ONE lifestyle choice you could put into action in your personal and professional lives that would bring about positive results.**

"So far, you've learned how to identify and eliminate unnecessary interference. You've identified your BIG ROCKS and tied roles and action items to them. We've worked together so you could build your own personal calendars. Now I want you to consider whether or not doing these things is going to help you build in those activities you described that, if you did them superbly well and consistently, would have significant positive results. I would also like you to consider what it is that you need to change in your life—if anything—to achieve balance."

I considered the question and reviewed my answers. It was clear to me that once again work had become the area in my life that needed to change so I could live according to my true priorities.

"Would anyone like to share their thoughts?" asked Bill.

Surprising even myself, I raised my hand.

"Yes, Jack," said Bill. "My volunteer from the rocks activity!"

"Thanks," I said. "Well, as I mentioned earlier, I'm an equities manager for a large company. I've only been at my job for about five months. Before that I worked in a similar position for another large company. I changed jobs because of long hours and feeling underappreciated.[1] I really thought that my new job was going to be different, and it was—at first. However, my hours have been steadily creeping up since I began, and I've recently been given a greater number of accounts, more than they originally told me I would have as a maximum. I'm beginning to feel as if I am right back in my old position. I'm feeling stressed, and once again I'm feeling pressure from my family about not spending enough time at home this summer. That's why I am here today.

"I learned about your workshop before I left my old job. However, the only solution I could see when I was working at my previous job was to leave. I thought finding a new job was the answer, and I really believed that I had asked all the right questions and found an environment that was a good fit. I was really excited about the new opportunity. Unfortunately, over the past month I've been feeling a lot of disappointment. I kept thinking about the advice I received from a man I met at my son's soccer game. He works for an organization that lives the BIG ROCKS strategy and was very enthusiastic about passing on the information. Maybe I should have attended one of these sessions earlier so I could have learned some new techniques for evaluating whether or not a new organization was the right fit for me. As I sit here and reflect on my life after what I've learned today, I'm not so sure I made the right choice about changing companies."

"Your story is familiar to me, Jack. Don't be so hard on yourself. As human beings we tend to be drawn into what is most comfortable or what is most familiar to us. It's common for us to repeat mistakes and find ourselves in similar situations to the ones we were trying to get out of.

"Consider what Albert Einstein once said about avoiding the repeating of mistakes and solving issues in your life. *'The significant problems we face cannot be solved at the same level of thinking we were at when we created them.'* In other words, if you want to solve your problems, you need to think about them from a different perspective—at a different level. That is what I am trying to do with this workshop—to get you to think about your life at a different level and look at it from a different perspective. As humans, we have the capability to do that.

"Jack, I would guess that you didn't talk to as many people in the new organization as you should have, and you maybe didn't notice some subtle clues about the working environment that are abundantly clear to you now. I would bet that if you sat down and made a list of the similarities and differences between the two companies, you would find more similarities than differences. My guess would also be that the companies are relatively the same size in terms of employees and revenue."

"That's true," I confirmed.

"My first piece of advice would be to go to a company that is completely different. Try interviewing at a place that you wouldn't normally choose. Seek out employment rather than looking for it to find you. Find a company that is involved in something you are interested in. Maybe you would consider working for a smaller company, something with a less rigid corporate structure than where you are now. That might mean that your job responsibilities could change a bit. You might have to do something different, but that could be a good thing. Be willing to be flexible and open to a completely new experience. What about the company that you mentioned was already living the BIG ROCKS strategy? Maybe there is an opportunity for you there, if you think their lifestyle may better match your needs."

"I don't know," I replied in a hedging way. "The company I was referring to was a sporting-goods company. I'm not so sure they would have an opportunity for me, but I see what you're saying."

"I think you should approach them, Jack. What have you got to lose? Every company needs folks with financial savvy and experience. I'm sure you could apply your skills in that regard, and it may challenge you to learn new things. Professional growth is never a bad thing! At the very least you may get a chance to talk to people who are living the BIG ROCKS strategy, and maybe they could provide you with other ideas. Also, don't 'settle' for a position if it doesn't meet all of your criteria. I understand that is difficult because you have bills to pay and a family to provide for. However, too many people settle for jobs that aren't right for them simply because they need the money. Research from Gallup clearly shows that eight out of ten employees are miscast in their roles. This is part of the reason why so many people struggle to find balance. Who really likes to do something all day long that they don't really enjoy? You have to find a job that you see as having more benefits than challenges. Be patient and wait for something that is the right fit for you. Give it some thought if you decide to make a job change.

"Another thing to consider is that maybe the company you work for now would be receptive to the BIG ROCKS strategy. I'd certainly be happy to talk to them or send you away with some materials to look at if you think it would help."

"Thanks," I said gratefully.

"I'd like to thank everyone for attending today. Recognizing that your life is out of balance and taking the initiative to attend this workshop to do something about it is a productive first step toward achieving balance in your lives. I hope you found the workshop worthwhile. My parting assignment for you today is to review what you've identified as your BIG ROCKS. Memorize what they are and then begin living according to your true priorities. To do that, you must complete your calendars and build in a small amount of time each day to keep them updated. Lastly, you need to identify and eliminate the interference in your life. Learn to say no! Actively living the BIG ROCKS strategy requires a daily commitment. Use your calendars and be diligent about keeping them current. The calendars serve as your lifestyle lifelines to managing your BIG ROCKS.

"I have one final question for you, and I would appreciate any feedback you have to offer. Can anyone give me one valuable thing you got out of today's workshop?"

"I'm amazed at how something so simple has made things so clear for me," said one person. "I just hope I can stick to it."

"The rocks activity was great. It really helped put things into perspective for me," said another.

"I think this workshop did exactly what you said. It forced me to invoke a new level of thinking—a new way of viewing my life. I like the quotes and all of the points that you made along the way. You reminded me of so many important things that I already knew but had neglected to keep at the forefront of my thinking," said another.

"I feel good about writing everything out. It definitely built a clearer picture of my life for me. This workshop helped me realize that I was really trying to cram too much into my life. I need to cut some things out and be more realistic with my time," added another.

"The worksheets, or the BIG ROCKS tools as you referred to them, are going to be very useful to me. I'm looking forward to getting the electronic versions of many of these so I can share them with my coworkers," said another.

"Great stuff," said Bill. "Each of you came here today looking for a new perspective and maybe a new way to gain the solutions to your current issues. Don't remain idle. Begin today to put the wheels in motion toward making the necessary changes in your life that allow you to actively live the BIG ROCKS strategy and be true to your life's priorities.

"Thanks for coming. I'll be available for the next half hour or so if you have further questions and would like to talk with me."

Following a round of applause, the room began to empty out. Several attendees stopped to ask questions and speak with Bill. I sat in my chair for several minutes reviewing my materials and thinking over what Bill had said about either seeking new employment or applying this strategy at my current company. I was on board with eliminating interference from my life. I just needed to decide how I would go about doing it. Lisa would no doubt be very helpful. I waited until I could ask Bill for the additional materials he had promised me to help approach my employers about the BIG ROCKS strategy, then gathered my belongings and headed home.

ELEVEN

Courage to Change

s I walked out to my car, I realized I was exhausted and exhilarated at the same time. I couldn't stop thinking about the rocks activity. I was amazed at how such a simple activity using rocks, pebbles, sand, and water had renewed and reshaped my perspective on my life. I now felt as though I had a clearer direction for how I wanted to implement changes in my life.

I felt very upbeat and positive at that moment. A lot of my enthusiasm had to do with all of the work I'd done today to identify my BIG ROCKS and build my calendars. Writing it all down made me feel more in control of my life and made me recognize that it was up to me to make the choices necessary to create my own preferred lifestyle. I had found that I was trying to fit too many things into my life, and, more importantly, I was trying to fit too many of the *wrong* things into my life. I was trying to fit in too many things that weren't even a priority for me. I was ready to try again using the BIG ROCKS strategy. I hoped this strategy and its tools would make the difference.

As I pulled onto the highway my thoughts veered toward what I should do about my job. I was still torn. Part of me thought I should just leave and start fresh. Yet there was another part of me that believed I owed it to my employers to tell them my needs and give them an opportunity to meet them. Maybe I would talk to them first. I thought I'd proven my value to the company, which would definitely provide me with some negotiating power.

One of my fellow workshop participants had made a great comment while we were building our calendars together. She had been an elementary school teacher at one point in her life, and she mentioned that equality in the classroom really boiled down to giving each child what he or she needed. It may not be the *same* thing for every child, but if you believed that all children were different based on their backgrounds, experiences, learning styles, interests, and abilities, then meeting their needs in an equal fashion equated to providing them each with different things. As she explained this concept, all I could think at the time was that it should be the same for any work environment, too. Our basic needs can't change that much as we become adults. I supposed that equality at work could be achieved by giving each employee what he or she needed as well. Personally speaking, I'd always been more motivated by receiving time off to spend with my family.[1] I knew of other employees who were more motivated by money, bonuses, or gifts to meet their needs. The best thing leaders could do to meet employees' needs would be to get to know them well enough to understand what motivated and inspired them. I imagined that required effective listening skills. Once you figured that out, then fully meeting their individual needs would be a lot easier. Maybe if I shared this information with my employers, they would be willing to listen to me and more fully meet my needs.

I realized the reality was that many employees' voices are never heard. I thought it was a sad irony that we lived in a democracy, yet most of the environments people chose to work in were anything but democratic. However, I had enough invested in this company now to give it a chance and see where it would lead. I had to develop a strategy, though, so I could go to my boss and state my case. Maybe I could even sell him on the BIG ROCKS strategy for the company as a whole. Bill had send me away with some extra materials, so I could pull everything together and present it to my boss. The worst he could say was no.

I was about halfway home, and my thoughts were still racing. I felt as I had that time at Jake's soccer game when Tom Baker told me about the BIG ROCKS strategy. My thoughts were going nonstop with all the information I'd taken in at the BIG ROCKS workshop. I was excited about what I'd learned, but it was really more than that. I couldn't wait to get home to Lisa and explain and talk through everything I'd learned and was now feeling. I knew she had been very frustrated because we'd had high hopes for some major changes about six months ago when I'd decided to make a job change. It hadn't worked out the way we'd planned, and in many respects, Lisa felt as if we were back to square one. This was my issue, and I was the only one who could solve it for myself. It was as Bill had said: we all need to take responsibility for ourselves and take action to make the changes necessary for achieving balance and alignment in our own lives.

How could I convince Lisa that this time was going to be different? How many times had she heard that before? This time, however, I could feel it. There was something about the way all of us at the workshop had been processed. That was what Bill had called it—"processed"—because he said we weren't being "taught," per se, but rather were being given tools and knowledge that we could apply to our own lives. It was as though Bill had given us a framework to let us make our own choices. He'd listened to our responses.

I was very involved and very inspired by Bill's approach, and I knew I could explain the concepts. I just wasn't sure I had the words to properly recapture the feeling I'd experienced going through the workshop. I couldn't wait to share those concepts with Lisa. She didn't know it yet, but she was going to be my sounding board. I was going to practice presenting this information to her, and then, based on her reaction, I was going to refine my "pitch" so I could present it to my boss.

As I got off at my exit, I tried to organize in my head the concepts that I'd taken away from the workshop. I thought the key points I needed to reiterate when it came to explaining the BIG ROCKS strategy centered on balance, alignment, and engagement. I knew I couldn't possibly walk into my boss's office and tell him that I had gone to a workshop where we played with rocks, pebbles, sand, and water. I needed to explain those central concepts of balance, alignment, and engagement. The first place I needed to start was balance and how I felt that my life was out of balance and out of alignment with my actual priorities. As a result, I was feeling disengaged, and I was trying to implement a strategy for myself that reengaged me. It certainly wasn't that I didn't like my work. I did like it, but I had so many accounts that I felt ineffective. I didn't have time to serve each customer the way they deserved to be served. This was draining the joy out of my work, not to mention the fact that other areas in my life were beginning to suffer because of the amount of time I needed to put into my work. As I reflected back on the workshop, I mentally organized the following list:

1. What is the BIG ROCKS strategy? A tool for achieving balance in my life

- Recognize and acknowledge that my life is out of balance
- Recognize that the most important things in my life are not getting the attention they deserve
- Recognize that the world we live and work in is different from the world our parents and/or grandparents lived and worked in

2. An explanation of the BIG ROCKS activity

- The significance of the six BIG ROCKS, the pebbles, sand, and water
- The reason why we put our rocks in first
- Identifying and eliminating interference
- Learning how to say no

3. The importance of identifying my BIG ROCKS, or my life's true priorities (no more than six)

- Committing to the true priorities in my life by identifying them and writing them down
- Alignment: matching up my true priorities with specific actions
- Associating specific roles and actions that I need to take to achieve balance in my life
- The majority of people don't include work as one of their top three BIG ROCKS

4. Developing weekly, monthly, and yearly calendars to keep my life in balance

- Writing everything down to get a clear picture of all the components of my life
- Working collaboratively; the value in teams
- Engagement, which leads to higher levels of productivity

That was all I could think of at the moment. I knew I'd have to pull out all of those statistics that Bill had presented to make the BIG ROCKS strategy clear for my boss. I'd do that over the weekend and then present it on Monday. The one thing I had to be extra careful about, however, was not to let on that I'd taken the workshop on my "sick day" off. My plan was to say I'd taken the

BIG ROCKS workshop during my transition week to make myself even more valuable as a new employee at CMC.

When I pulled into my driveway, I turned off the engine and got out to greet my children, who were running out the front door to see their dad. When I walked into the house, the first thing I did after I said hello to everyone was line up a sitter for the children and make plans for a quiet dinner out with my wife. It wasn't that I didn't want to spend time with my kids, but right then I really needed to have Lisa to myself so she could fully listen and help me sort out not only what I'd learned today but also the best direction for me to take. My decisions affected her most of all, and she sometimes knew me better than I knew myself. She would help me make the best choices for our family and myself. Lisa and I actually waited and went to dinner at 8 P.M. so we could spend an hour with our children before we left. Lisa was surprised at my spontaneity in getting a sitter and whisking her off to dinner alone. Bill had said you had to leave room in your bowls for spontaneity, so there you had it.

"That must have been some workshop you went to today!" Lisa said jokingly. "Should I sign you up for one every week?"

I laughed and said, "If that's what it takes for me to feel this reenergized about my life, I just might sign myself up for one of these workshops every week. I'm not sure if it's in our family budget, though. It was a great day, and I'd like to learn more, but first I need to digest everything I learned today, and I want to share it with you. I want to try out this new strategy—called BIG ROCKS—and see if it works for me and if it meets your needs and our family's, too. I know that the past six months have been a real struggle for you, Lisa."

As she sat and listened to me, I knew what Lisa was thinking because we'd had this conversation many times before. She'd also considered leaving her job in order to make the family run more smoothly, but we'd both decided that it wasn't the answer. Lisa needed to work, too, and she needed to pursue her own career to fulfill her dreams. Also, our family needed the second income. The real issue was that I worked too many hours.

As I began to explain everything that had transpired that day, I could sense that Lisa was beginning to warm up to my newfound enthusiasm. I knew, too, that she'd still have reservations about all this until I actually put it into action.

I tried to ease Lisa's concerns as I reached over the table to hold her hand.

"I feel bad about the frustrations I cause you and the kids, Lisa. That's why I want to get your take on the information I learned today by sharing some of the work I did in the workshop with you. You've always been able to see things more clearly than me. I wish you could have gone to this workshop because it put so many things into perspective for me. Not only that, but it also gave me some very helpful tools that will make me more successful in balancing my life's true priorities."

Lisa and I talked for a long time about what I'd learned. I explained about balance, alignment, and engagement; the BIG ROCKS activity; and eliminating interference. I barely even touched the dinner I'd ordered because I was so busy talking.

"I don't remember seeing you this enthusiastic about something since I told you I was pregnant with Beckie," Lisa pointed out laughingly. "You've really developed a passion for this strategy in only one day? Are you sure it's going to work?"

"I'm going to make sure it works," I told her. "I identified my priorities today, and then I came up with things to do that would support my priorities. I'm actually living this new strategy right now. My biggest priority—or BIG ROCK—is you, and this time together tonight is part of my plan to infuse balance into our life. I even created several calendars to lay out a plan to continue living this every day."

I showed Lisa my calendars, and after looking at them, she asked if I had extra copies of the worksheets so she could sit down later at home and create her own. "Maybe it will be more helpful if we could synch our schedules and be responsible together for building in more time for one another and the children," she said. "Maybe you could walk me through the process at home."

I agreed to do that. I was grateful that my wife was being so supportive. This activity reminded me why I had married her. She'd always been willing to jump in and do what was best for our family and make improvements when they were needed.

At one point during our conversation, I asked Lisa what her BIG ROCKS were. She thought carefully about it before she responded, "Well … definitely you first, then the kids, my parents, my friends, my health, and my job. I think that's it." She gave me the smile I'd loved most about her since I'd met her. Lisa and I left the restaurant feeling a renewed sense of hope.

When I returned to work on Monday, I scheduled a meeting with my supervisor for the following Monday to share all I'd learned with him. I needed a little time to prepare.

During the week, Lisa helped me come to a decision about how to eliminate the interference that my work was creating for me. We weighed the pros and cons about staying in my current job. Ultimately, I was going to be honest with my boss about my needs. I was going to tell him that I felt my expectations were not being met according to what I had believed about this position from the initial interview. Then I was going to tell him about this new strategy and how I planned to adopt it for myself. We'd see where it went from there. I really wanted to stay in this job if they could be supportive of my new life strategy. However, my backup plan was to do some research to begin looking for another position with another company in case this didn't work out.

Over the weekend before the big meeting, I organized my thoughts and prepared copies of my workshop materials. I organized some of the statistics Bill had presented to strengthen my case.

Late Sunday evening I sat in my living room with the TV off, alone with my thoughts. I was starting to feel very nervous. There was something about confronting my boss and possibly creating conflict that brought out the five-year-old child in me. It was a fear of the unknown, I supposed. My boss's reaction was going to determine my future, and if I were forced into making the choice to seek new employment, that would bring about another pile of issues.

"What's wrong?" asked Lisa, startling me.

"I'm just thinking about tomorrow," I told her.

"You're nervous. I can tell."

"Yes. I'm just hoping I say all the right things. I don't want to leave anything out. I want him to understand. I want him to be supportive. I want …"

"Stop for a minute," Lisa said soothingly as she placed her hand on my shoulder. "All you have to do to calm your nerves about tomorrow is to remember why you are doing this. You are doing this because you are tired of working too many hours, tired of being taken advantage of because you're good at what you do, tired of leaving late because you're afraid of being noticed as the first one out the door. You're tired of missing important events in your children's lives, tired of missing life with your family and friends, and most of all, you're just plain tired. I need you to do this, Jack—for you … for us. I need you to regain your old energy and sense of passion about life. I need you to be more involved in our lives and find a better balance. I saw a big change in you after the BIG ROCKS workshop. Don't lose that momentum now."

"You're right, and I know it," I responded. "I just feel very strongly that what I'm going to present can help others in the company if I can gain my boss's support, but I just don't know if he *will* support me."

"Stop worrying about it, Jack. You can't control his reaction. If he doesn't get on board with the same level of enthusiasm, then it's his loss. Don't let that affect you. If he doesn't support you, then it's not the right place for you. The kids and I support you, and that's all that really matters. Come on, let's go to bed. Get your rest so you'll be fresh for tomorrow."

Monday morning came, and I passed on my usual tea to keep my nerves in check. When I got to work, I gathered my materials and knocked on my boss's door. I'd brought my calendars along to show him how I planned to make the BIG ROCKS strategy work for me.

"Thanks for meeting with me, Ian," I said. We talked briefly about a few key financial recommendations for several of my clients. According to Ian, I was doing a good job and the company was happy with my performance. I thanked him for the feedback and then began my pitch.

"Actually, Ian, I wanted to talk with you about several challenges I'm facing right now, and I'm hoping to have your support. Back when I interviewed for this job, one of the things that impressed me most was the value placed on family and outside interests. I came away from the interview feeling very excited about working in this environment. Although I really believe that everyone here embraces those values, I just find myself struggling with all the hours I feel compelled to put in to get my work done.

"I was originally told that each account representative would have no more than forty-five accounts to manage. I already have fifty-two, which is why I have to work so much overtime. I want to avoid a situation like I had at my last job, where it became difficult to get out of the office because I was never caught up. I'm trying really hard right now to balance everything in my life. My personal life suffered when I worked at my last company because of the demands of my job. I really like working here at CMC, Ian. I like what I do, and I like the people. Most importantly, I really feel that I add value to the company. I just want to discuss this with you now before things get out of hand." I could feel my body tensing up as I spoke.

Ian leaned back in his chair and put his fingertips together, cocked his head to one side, and looked at me intently for a few seconds. It only took those few seconds for me to start figuring out my quickest escape from his office … straight to the unemployment line. I began to sweat.

"I see where you're coming from, Jack. I actually appreciate you speaking to me. Obviously, I don't want there to be any issues either. So far you have done a fantastic job for us, and we're very happy with your performance. You're absolutely right, you do add value to our company."

I'm sure Ian could see my body literally sag with relief at his words as I glanced up quickly to offer a quick prayer of thanks. His reaction wasn't bad at all … better than I could have hoped for.

I took a deep breath and soldiered on. I began telling Ian all about BIG ROCKS. To his credit, he listened to me and reviewed all the materials as I explained them. The meeting concluded after two hours, and after a moment of reflection, Ian said, "Very interesting idea, Jack, I'll take it under consideration." However, my joy and relief at the conclusion of this meeting were short-lived as he added, "By the way, do you think you're still on track to meet your targets this month?"

As he said those words, I felt as if my stomach were dropping to the floor. It wasn't so much the question itself because it was a reasonable concern, considering my job responsibilities. It just wasn't the time to be asking it. It was as though he hadn't heard a word I'd said. I did a quick look around to make sure I wasn't sitting back at my old office at Rutter. I told him that I was going to not only meet but likely exceed my targets this month, and then I went back to my desk to get some work done and was out the door by 5 P.M. I was feeling pretty good about myself and had no regrets about sharing my needs with Ian.

When I got home, I recounted my meeting to Lisa, and she said all we could do now was wait and see how my boss responded to my ideas.

At 4 P.M. the next afternoon, Ian e-mailed me his response:

Thanks so much for the meeting yesterday, Jack. I really appreciate your honesty and candor. Thanks, too, for sharing the BIG ROCKS strategy and information. I want to respond to you on two issues:

1. First, as it relates to the number of accounts that you handle. I am relieving you of two accounts so that you will now handle only fifty. I can't eliminate any more than that at this time. If we gain enough business over the

next six to eight months, then we can hire another equities manager. At that point we can decrease the number of accounts you have by five more. Although it won't totally eliminate all the overtime you're putting in, I hope it helps a little bit. Given the great job you do on all your existing accounts, we have faith in your ability to handle this workload.

2. Second, as it relates to BIG ROCKS. I enjoyed hearing about the strategy. I can see its validity, and I was impressed with your enthusiasm. However, at this time when we are approaching summer, traditionally a down time for the market, our customers are going to need our time first and foremost. Therefore, now would not be the best time to attempt to implement a strategy such as BIG ROCKS. However, I am going to hold on to all of the materials that you gave me and revisit this strategy in January. By then we should be able to hire another equities manager, which will alleviate the pressure on everyone, meaning that we will have more time to commit to this should we decide to move forward. Of course, I will have to share this information with the executive team and get their approval before we adopt the BIG ROCKS strategy.

Thanks again, Jack, for your initiative. I hope transitioning the two accounts away from you is helpful. Keep up the great work!

Best Regards—Ian

I reread the e-mail to make sure I hadn't missed anything. I actually managed my disappointment better than I had thought I would. I guessed a part of me had already known what the outcome would be. I'd actually figured out fairly early on that Ian was a "bottom line" kind of boss. My instincts had just been confirmed, and it didn't take me long to realize that CMC wasn't the place for me. I was now more committed than ever to trying to find a company that would support my lifestyle. I realized it would take at least the next six to eight months to find a new job … if I was lucky. If by chance I was still at CMC in January, then I'd make sure the BIG ROCKS strategy idea was brought up again. Being realistic, though, I wasn't going to wait and hope that everything worked out. I had done that at Rutter and ended up waiting four years longer than I should have for changes to be made. They never were. I couldn't take that chance again. I needed to take control and do this for me … for my family … and for my sanity. Another life transition; here I went again. I hoped Lisa would take this news well.

TWELVE

Facing the Truth

L et's go to dinner with the kids tonight," I said to Lisa as soon as I walked in the door, planning on breaking the news to her. "How about pizza?"

"Sounds great," she said, knowing full well that the kids would eat and then play some video games in the back of the restaurant. While they were having fun, we'd get a chance to talk. I wanted to share the e-mail that Ian had sent me and strategize about our next move.

Lisa made a comment about my being home early because it was only 5:30 P.M. "I'm right on time," I whispered with a smile. "BIG ROCKS, remember? I am making a commitment to always be home for dinner, and I'm sticking to it. It's one of my non-negotiable action items." Lisa smiled, fully understanding what I meant by that, and went to get ready for dinner.

I was trying to be true to my BIG ROCKS calendar. I had work on my desk I could have stayed to finish, but it would just have to keep until tomorrow. I was going to do the best I could with the time I had. I'd been diligent about helping Lisa get the kids ready and out the door for school, so I hadn't been going in early. However, in a few weeks the kids would be out of school and we would have our summer babysitter in the mornings, giving me the extra time I needed to go to work earlier and keep my work caught up. I wanted to do a respectable job in my position until I moved on, but I was also committed to keeping the balance.

We arrived at the pizza restaurant and ordered a couple of pizzas. While waiting for our food, Lisa and I listened to Jake and Beckie tell us about their exciting last few days of school. We discussed their summer plans and tried to get answers about anything special that they would like to do. We were going to spend a week at the beach in early August and were looking forward

to that. I knew there were also two camps—soccer and baseball—that Jake
was interested in, and I knew Beckie wanted to go to both a basketball and
a summer dance camp with her friends. The food arrived, and we continued
chatting while we ate. Just as we expected, Jake and Beckie cleaned us out of
quarters and went to play video games. Lisa and I now had a chance to talk.

"Ian e-mailed me today in response to our meeting," I told Lisa.

"He sent you an e-mail?" she asked, visibly put off. "Why couldn't he tell
you in person?"

"I don't know," I sighed as I handed Lisa the e-mail. I waited while she
read it, feeling like a kid showing his mom a bad report card.

"Well I guess that's that, Jack; your backup plan is going into effect," said
Lisa decisively. "You're looking for a new job. Are you still all right with that?"

"Yes, and I'm going to follow Bill's advice."

"Bill? Oh, the BIG ROCKS guy. What do you mean?" she asked.

"I'm going to do the research this time and identify the companies I'd like
to work for, and then I'm going to approach them regardless of whether or
not they have a position available. My goal is going to be finding companies
that fit my lifestyle. I'm going to look for places that fit my professional *and*
personal interests. Then I'm going to do things differently because I'm going
to interview the companies instead of them interviewing me. I'm also going
to look at smaller companies. I always go after the large financial institutions
because that's what I'm comfortable with and what I know. Unfortunately,
that comfort zone has landed me in the same situation twice—well, three
times, actually, if I count the job I had before Rutter. I'm going to change my
behavior so I don't make the same mistakes again. I'm also going to look at
companies that operate in industries other than finance. After all, every company needs financial management of some kind, right?"

"I think that's a great idea," said Lisa. "Not to burst your bubble, but how
are you going to determine if the company you choose will fit your lifestyle?"

"I have some thoughts on that, and maybe you can help talk me through
them. First of all, I'm going to talk to a lot of people who work at the company before I accept a position. I think I made a lot of mistakes when I took
my current job at Columbia Management Company. Good ol' CMC isn't
exactly what I thought it would be. Things were so bad at Rutter I just
wanted out, and that made me jump at the first thing that was offered to me.
I saw what I wanted to see at CMC because I felt any place would be better
than Rutter, and that was the wrong approach.

"Also, when I interviewed at CMC, I thought I asked all the right questions. I asked about the executives' views on family and outside interests, and I was impressed when one of them said he never misses his kid's games. Well, of course he doesn't; he's one of the executives. There isn't anyone telling him what to do. I've realized that I did ask all the right questions, but where I went wrong was that I didn't ask all the right people. I should have spoken to other equities managers and administrative staff as well as some of their customers to get a better feel for the lifestyle of the company. I should have asked some of the employees questions like how well they worked together. I should have looked around and paid closer attention to employee interactions. I could have asked if any of the employees saw one another outside work. I should have asked about company events, or even sat in the parking lot to see what happened at 5 o'clock. Did everyone leave on time? How late did they stay? Things like that."

"I think what you're saying is that you should have gotten to know them on a more personal level before you accepted the job," Lisa suggested. "Don't you think that would be difficult to do?"

"Maybe, but at least I could have asked the questions. If people didn't respond or if they were cold and reserved in their responses, then I guess I would have had my answer. If it truly were a great place to work, the majority of the people I talked to would have said that. Look, I understand that no place is perfect, but that's not the issue. I need to find a job that will be right for me. That's the difference. I need to do my homework to find the right companies. I think the real key is to do up-front research before I start knocking on doors. If I find the right companies and then go in and ask the right questions, I think that'll be my best chance to land a position that supports my lifestyle. I know I have my work cut out for me, but I'm going to give it a go."

Lisa looked at me thoughtfully for a moment and then asked, "Have you thought that if your plan is to seek out companies that match your lifestyle, we may have to move? I mean, what are the chances of you finding exactly what you want within, say, an hour's drive?"

"I hadn't really thought of that, but I guess it is something that we may have to consider," I said.

"I'm not sure I'm really on board with that," commented Lisa. "I mean, don't get me wrong, I'm willing to make a lot of sacrifices, but I love my job. I have great benefits working for the state, and my counseling position really fits our family schedule very well. Also, I love our home, and most importantly, our children are established here and are really involved with sports and their friends. Our town has a great school system, too. I don't think it would be fair to uproot the kids right now."

"I completely agree with you, Lisa, and, trust me, it's the last thing I want to do. All I'm saying is that I don't think we should completely close the door on it if the right opportunity presents itself. I promise that my first round of research will begin locally and branch out from there."

"Fair enough," conceded Lisa.

All of a sudden I heard a voice behind me: "Jack. Jack Bedford, how are ya, guy?" Lisa looked up, and I turned to see my friend Tom Baker from the soccer field approaching our table.

"Hi, Tom! I'm well. Thanks for asking," I said as I shook Tom's hand. "How are you doing?"

"Things are great. I'm just gearing up for summer. Are you sending Jake to soccer camp at the rec center this summer? They're having a Major League Soccer camp this year. I think Jake would get a lot out of it."

"Yep, we'll be there! In fact, we were just discussing that over dinner. Come have a seat with us for a minute. Tom, this is my wife, Lisa. Lisa, this is Tom Baker. Tom is Chris Baker's father. Chris plays on Jake's soccer team. Actually, Tom is the guy who introduced me to the BIG ROCKS strategy!"

Lisa greeted Tom, who asked, "Did you ever get a chance to attend a workshop, Jack?"

"Yeah, actually I did just two weeks ago. Things at my new job had been starting to feel too much like my old job. Remember, I told you all about how I was leaving one company for a new job the last time we spoke?" Tom nodded. "Well, anyway, I took it upon myself to attend the BIG ROCKS workshop and start making some changes. I tried to sell my current boss on the idea, and although he seemed receptive, he ultimately said that the timing was off and that we should revisit the information next January."

Tom suggested, "You should recommend that he and other executives attend the workshop to really gain a better understanding of all the BIG ROCKS concepts, just like I told you when I introduced you to BIG ROCKS. And look at the bright side: at least your boss didn't give you a flat-out 'no.'"

"That's true," I agreed. "I'm just not so sure I'm willing to wait around until he makes up his mind. I'm really struggling again. I mean, I have a much better grasp on my schedule because I'm using the tools I got from the BIG ROCKS workshop. You know, the ROCKS sheets and the calendars. I've mapped out a plan, and, to be fair to myself, I am really trying to stick to it. However, I just see my calendar coming into conflict with the volume of work I have at my job. I'm struggling to squeeze fitness into my schedule, and because of that I'm starting to gain weight again. I'd lost seventeen pounds and now I've gained nine back. Do you have any openings at CSAN?" I asked Tom.

"Well, don't laugh, Jack. We just might. Right now we don't have any openings. It's a great place to work, and the company is really growing. However, we are working on a partnership deal that will create a new division if all goes according to plan. The new division would focus on selling sporting equipment and apparel to the general public. As you know, right now we only focus on large equipment deals to schools, rec centers, sports teams, and the like. This move would expand our business, and I know it would require some new accounting procedures. If it happens, we'll need someone with your expertise—or what I believe is your expertise—to manage the financials," Tom said.

"I do have that expertise, and I can be flexible in the way I use my talent as long as someone is willing to give me a chance," I offered.

"I'll tell you what, Jack, if we decide to move forward with creating the new division and decide to hire, I'll give you a call and at least get you an interview. Remember, for us it's about you fitting in with our lifestyle. We typically use several learning-style inventories and talent profiles to assure the best fit with our company. Basically, what I'm saying is that I can't give you any guarantees, but I can get you a foot in the door," explained Tom.

"That's more than I could ask for, Tom. Thanks."

"Well, on that note, I think my pizza is ready. I've got to get this food home. I have hungry kids waiting, so things could turn ugly real fast," Tom said with a chuckle. "Lisa, it was great to meet you, and, Jack, best of luck to you."

"Nice to meet you, too," said Lisa as she extended her hand.

"Thanks, Tom. Great to see you," I said as Tom walked to get his pizza. I watched as he stopped to say hello to Jake and Beckie, and then he was out the door.

"Well, that was a coincidence," Lisa said with a glint of hope in her eyes. "You never know."

Just then Jake and Beckie came running over looking for more quarters.

"Enough video games," Lisa and I said in unison. "We need to be getting home." I paid the check, and we all headed home.

THIRTEEN

The
BIG ROCKS
Payoff

Once everyone was settled in back at home, I sat down at the computer to begin job hunting. I made a mental note to schedule "job hunting" into my calendar, since I knew this would be something I'd be doing just about every night for quite some time.

I began my search using the Internet to dig out broad articles that discussed some of the best companies to work for in my region. Once I came up with a handful of company names, I expanded my search by looking for any press coverage on each company that focused on topics that were employee-related as well as stories that discussed customer care or goodwill initiatives. After two hours of searching, I was getting tired. "That's enough for tonight," I thought. "I'll continue with more research tomorrow."

Over the next week or so I spent several hours online looking for companies I could pursue. I combed through my state's website and different Chamber of Commerce chapters to see what information I could find. I searched through several local and regional papers—not the Help Wanted section but the business section to review different business profiles. I even contacted two local newspaper business writers to see if they could provide any leads.

On Saturday I went to the library to get some help searching for any national, regional, and state lists that ranked companies according to the best places to work. I primarily searched through newspapers and recent business magazines. I wanted to get the most current information that I could.

By early the next week, I'd identified seven companies that could be a potential fit. The longest potential commute would be two hours each way. Not too bad, but I would prefer to keep it under an hour—or maybe this company would be open to my working from home a few days per week. I spent the next two weeks preparing my résumé and cover letters for each company. I was planning to hand-deliver all of them so that I would get a chance to poke around and check the companies out a little bit. I was diligent about personalizing each cover letter. Next, I began delivering my résumés in order according to how high I had placed each company on my priority list. I could only do one per day because I was trying to do it on my lunch hour or immediately following my workday when I could leave a little early.

The search process had taken me over a month, but I was proud of myself because even though I was creating extra work for myself, I was also managing to live by my BIG ROCKS calendars fairly diligently. On the downside, I was feeling a bit overwhelmed because my work was piling up as a result of not putting in so much overtime. This week I was planning to go in early every day to clear up the extra work. I could do this because the kids were finally out of school and the 4th of July weekend was fast approaching. I had an extra day off due to the holiday the following week, and I was really excited because I'd landed an interview on that day. Because so many companies had different interviewing processes, I had no idea how long this first interview would take, but Lisa took the day off, too, in the hope that I'd be home before noon and we could spend the rest of the day with the kids.

I was hoping to get at least one more interview scheduled for that day, but I guessed I needed to be patient. None of the companies had any openings except the one that had called me for an interview, which was a large drugstore chain. That was just luck, I figured. There was one company that manufactured golf equipment that I was really impressed by. I'd hoped they would call, and if they didn't I still planned to be diligent about following up each month or so to see if anything had opened up. At the very least it would get them to pull my résumé out again. For that golf company in particular, however, I planned to drop in every now and then.

On the day of my interview with the drugstore company, I wasn't even nervous. I'd really changed my thinking about the whole interview process. I was interviewing them, I thought. I had my checklist tucked discreetly into my notepad because I wanted to make sure I looked for clues about the company lifestyle. I knew I was meeting with two or three people from 8 A.M. to 10 A.M. Afterward, I was going to ask if I could look around.

I wanted to take the opportunity to introduce myself to several other employees to see if I could engage them in brief conversations. I wanted to observe employee interactions if at all possible.

I walked into the lobby of the office building and asked for Mr. Rick Hillenbrand. I waited in the lobby for ten minutes, and he came to greet me just a few minutes after 8 A.M. He brought me up to the third floor, and I followed him down several corridors past numerous offices and into a fairly small conference room. There I was introduced to Dave Walker, who said, "Jack, Steve Capelli was supposed to join us this morning as well, but he was called out to a meeting. Please accept our apologies."

"No problem," I said, and the interview began with Rick providing a brief introduction to the company. Dave followed with a detailed description about the position itself. He handed me a folder that included corporate policies, a formal job description, and company training requirements and opportunities. As the interview moved on from there, I was impressed with the fact that both men began by asking me personal questions about my interests and myself. The questions were asked in a very generic way so I felt comfortable giving as much or as little information as I wanted. This made the interview less formal and opened the door for us to get to know one another on a more personal level. I made sure to ask them the same questions in return. Something Bill shared with us about building friendships at work had stuck with me. I was trying to decide whether or not either of these guys possessed the characteristics that would make them a good "friend." Did they seem like they were dependable and honest? I wondered. Did they seem like they would be easy to work with? Were they team players? Would I fit in with them? Were these guys I could see myself going out for a drink with?

The interview moved through work-related questions about my skills and experience. This part was fairly typical. Next, Rick and Dave turned the floor over to me and asked if there was anything I would like to add or any questions I would like to ask.

I asked for clarification of a few points regarding the job and the company, and inquired about the possibility of working from home a couple days per week to alleviate the pressure of the commute. I wanted them to fully understand my needs. I talked briefly about the BIG ROCKS strategy. Dave had actually heard of it from a friend who had attended the workshop, which worked out great because the conversation became lively at that point. I ended up talking about it for twenty minutes, and although we'd gone over our allotted time, neither Rick nor Dave tried to move me along. Instead they listened patiently and became actively involved in the conversation. Finally we were done talking, and Rick handed me two talent profiles to fill out.

"There are no right and wrong answers," said Rick. "We just want to get a feel for your talents and abilities and understand how your skills would complement the team you'd be working with. We ask all of our employees to complete these talent profiles. Let us know if you have any questions as you fill them out."

Rick and Dave left the conference room to give me enough time to complete the profiles. When I finished, I went to find Rick. I handed him my profiles and asked if he minded either giving me a tour or just letting me look around for a short time. He gave me a tour, and I took notice of the office spaces of many employees. There were lots of pictures up in offices. As we walked around, I asked Rick if he knew the company's annual attrition rate.

"I don't know the exact number, but I do know that it's low. We can stop by Jan's desk in HCM later on to get the exact percentage if you'd like."

"HCM?" I asked.

"Oh, sorry. HCM is short for Human Capital Management. In our organization, our HCM department is at the forefront. Just as it is important to manage our business finances effectively, we believe in managing our people effectively by being diligent about meeting their needs. We look at all of our employees as assets—human capital."

I nodded and gave him an approving, raised-eyebrow look as Rick went on to point out numerous employees who'd worked for the company for more than a decade. I was fortunate that the last stop on my office tour was in the third-floor break room. I smiled as I noticed several employees enjoying a cup of coffee together. Rick was introducing me to a few folks when we heard him being paged over the intercom system to take a call.

"This will only be a minute, Jack. If you don't mind waiting here for just a few minutes, I promise I'll be right back."

"This is perfect timing," I thought. I now had a little time to speak with these employees out of Rick's hearing. I asked them how they liked working for the company, and I was impressed with their enthusiastic answers. Based on what they said, I felt they were genuinely happy. It was evident that they felt valued because one of the women excitedly shared that she'd been recognized for the Swanee Award the previous month. I wasn't quite sure what that was, but she sure seemed happy to have it, and her colleagues were teasing her because they hadn't gotten it that month. There seemed to be a good rapport among the group, which I took as a very positive sign. In fact, one woman I spoke with had a son who went to school with Jake. I asked her how she managed the commute because it had taken me a little under two hours to get there for the interview. She said she didn't particularly like the commute, but the trade-off was that she loved her job. I asked if I could give her a call later to talk more about the company if she didn't mind, and she agreed without hesitation. It also occurred to me that we might be able to carpool if this turned out to be the right opportunity for me.

We all talked for a few more minutes before Rick returned. I shook his hand and thanked him for the interview. He told me that he'd be in touch within the next two weeks.

I began my drive home at 11 A.M., feeling really good about the company, the people, and the interview. Lisa was anxiously waiting to hear how it had gone. I called her from the car to fill her in.

"Sounds promising," she said. "It must be your lucky day!"

"Why's that?" I asked. "Because I had a good interview?"

"Well, yes, and also your friend Tom Baker called this morning."

"What did he say?" I asked, intrigued.

"Well, apparently that partnership that he mentioned is a go. CSAN signed a formal deal, and they are now moving forward with creating a new division. He said he and six of his colleagues would like to meet with you Friday afternoon at 1 P.M. if you can manage it. Tom said the interview would likely last the entire afternoon, so you'd have to take the afternoon off work. Do you think you could manage that?" asked Lisa, sounding a bit concerned.

"I'll figure out a way to make it work," I told her emphatically. "I'll be home in two hours. Why don't you get the kids ready and I'll change quickly so we can head out and enjoy the beach for the rest of the day. We'll pick up some sandwiches and drinks on the way."

"Sounds like a plan," she said with a smile in her voice as she hung up.

It really *must* be my lucky day, I thought. As they say, when it rains, it pours. I was really grateful that Tom had remembered to call me and had enough confidence in me to get me the interview. I couldn't wait to meet with them to see what they'd have to offer. For the first time in a long time,

I forgot about my job concerns as I relaxed and enjoyed the rest of the day with my family.

On the Friday morning of my interview at CSAN, I went to CMC early so I could get as much of my work done as possible. I'd taken the afternoon off by requesting personal time. I wasn't sure why I'd be meeting with this group for five hours; it seemed like a long time for a first interview. Nonetheless, I was excited about the opportunity. From what Tom had said, this position seemed very entrepreneurial, and I would have a great deal of input in developing the new division. I was excited because I'd had a lot of experience with market penetration and return ratios. I knew I could be very valuable to this initiative. I just hoped that they would be willing to look beyond my lack of experience in their industry and recognize that my skills could easily be developed. Taking the interview at this company was a big change of direction for me. I'd only worked for large financial organizations. This was a much smaller, privately owned company in a completely different industry.

I left work and arrived at Tom's company fifteen minutes early. Even though I was early, the owner, Garrett McLean, immediately came out to greet me. He invited me into the conference room and offered me something to drink and eat. "We always seem to have food laid out in this room. I'm not sure if it's a good or bad thing," he said laughingly, patting his stomach. "Help yourself and get comfortable. I want to give you an overview of the company and then give you a rundown of what you can expect from this interview today."

I settled in my chair, and Garrett began a formal presentation using slides, which pointed out that the company put a lot of thought and effort into its hiring practices. "The first question we have to ask ourselves as a company is, 'Do we have all of the right people working together within our organization?' Now, when I say 'the right people,' I'm looking at it from multiple perspectives.

"First, I want to know if all my people have the same work ethic. Next, I want to make sure they share the same belief system with everyone already working in the organization. Third, I want to make sure the person understands how the company operates and that it is an organization of choice. Fourth, I want to make sure that any position is the right role for the person we choose to hire. We do that by assessing your work habits, working style, and personal strengths. Before you leave I will have you complete some talent profiles to identify your individual strengths," explained Garrett. "Also, later on today you'll meet many of the people who work here so they can share their perspectives on our company with you. If we offer you a position and you accept, our goal is to make sure that you have enough information about our people and us that you can make a decision to accept a position here at CSAN with a high degree of confidence.

"The purpose behind profiling potential employees to uncover their talents and strengths is to help us build better teams. We work hard to make sure we utilize all of our people's talents and skills most effectively. We need to ask ourselves, are we providing the opportunity for each employee's strengths and talents to emerge, grow, and thrive? If we do that, then we ensure the highest level of success for our company and, more importantly, for the individual people involved in making it run effectively and efficiently.

"Like I said, in a little while I'll give you several different profiles to complete. We want to find out about you, your personality type, learning style, talents, and strengths. Our goal today is to find out if you are one of the right people for our organization. Will your strengths be a strong complement to the strengths of your teammates? Keep in mind, Jack, that we want you to evaluate us as well. Are we opening the right door for you? Does our company fit your lifestyle? I know from speaking with Tom that you're familiar with what we mean when we use the term 'lifestyle.' Is this right?"

"Yes, I actually attended a workshop with Bill Conley called BIG ROCKS, and we learned about lifestyles and how they're different from cultures," I said. "As I understand it, cultures are imposed from the top down, whereas lifestyles are created by everyone involved."

"Well stated," said Garrett. "I just wanted to make sure I was being clear. We have adopted so much of the language of BIG ROCKS and lifestyles that it's second nature for me to use the terms. However, I always want to be sure that I'm clearly getting my message across and not confusing you in any way.

"We ask that you fill out three instruments during this interview, Jack. We use a number of different instruments here, but we believe that the three we use in the interview process best help us to get to know you. Don't be surprised if some of the people you meet today share the same talents and strengths as you. Actually, we make sure we employ a diversity of strengths and talents that complement each other. We also make sure all employees exercise their strengths and talents as often as possible. This serves two purposes. First, it allows people to feel good about themselves because they are being asked to do things that they are good at, and second, the company winds up receiving quality work. I firmly believe that none of us are as smart as all of us."

I nodded and smiled and waited for Garrett to continue. He walked me through the rest of his slides, focusing primarily on his employees. He talked about using the communication processes for alignment and engagement that were learned as part of Bill Conley's approach. I asked questions that helped me get a handle on how much autonomy employees had. I wanted to find out if CSAN supported flexible working hours. I was surprised at Garrett's answers. He told me that everyone managed his or her own schedule and that as long as they got their work done, they could arrange their schedules as they saw fit.

"I also believe in giving my employees a lot of responsibility," said Garrett. "One of the things I often say to people who come to me to make a decision is, 'If I have to tell you what to do, then why do I need you?' Now, when you first hear that, it may sound harsh, but I don't mean it that way. What I mean when I say that to an employee is, 'I trust your judgment,' and 'I am confident that you know the best decision to make in most situations.' I expect every employee to take on a specific level of responsibility and make the appropriate decisions."

"What if I don't know what to do in a given situation or I don't know my level of responsibility, as you put it?" I asked.

"You can always ask my opinion. My door is always open. Also, Jack, please understand that there is a learning curve for each new employee when it comes to knowing his or her individual levels of responsibility. If you are ever unsure about whether or not it is your place to make a given decision, simply ask me, 'Is this my level of responsibility?' I will tell you yes or no, and if you do this often enough, and as we get to know each other better, you will eventually learn your own level of responsibility. In a participatory environment where our company goal is to provide our employees with choice, it is expected that it will take time for each employee to learn."

Garrett went on to tell me about the company's mission and goals. Next he asked me what my core values were. At first I wasn't sure how to answer because no one had ever asked me this before. My puzzled look prompted Garrett to explain further.

"Jack, what I'm asking you to do is to look within yourself and tell me the core values that you choose to live by. These would be the values that you would most want to pass on to your children. They are the values that guide you through life—your moral compass, so to speak, or the values that you subscribe to that can be reflected in decisions you make in your life."

I thought for a moment, and two immediately came to mind. "Well, respect and trust are two of my core values," I said to Garrett.

"Great. Now, let me share with you our corporate core values. Keep in mind that I didn't come up with these. The people who work here collectively came up with our core values. They are what drive all of our corporate decisions and they are Respect, Integrity, Caring, Honesty, Trust, and Discipline. Have you noticed that two of your core values match ours? This is definitely a positive sign."

Garrett asked me to write CSAN's corporate core values down so I could give them further thought. "If you join our team, we need to be sure that you subscribe to, and truly believe in, our core values. We try very hard to live by them every day." Lastly, Garrett provided me with a brief company history and information on the new division I could potentially be heading and asked if I had any questions.

I didn't have any questions because I'd been asking them as we went along. I told Garrett I was impressed with everything I'd heard so far and truly appreciated the opportunity to have met him. He told me how important he believed it was for him to be involved in every aspect of his employees' development and reemphasized his focus on team values. He talked about corporate procedures for ensuring that each employee had adequate opportunities for training in order to enhance both professional and personal growth. He also talked about his own background in sports, and it suddenly clicked with me why team values were so important to him. That was when I truly began to believe in what he was saying and to trust him.

The rest of the interview went by quickly. I took the three profiles to determine my talents, strengths, and learning style, and I met nine other employees. I was very comfortable during the entire interview. I also felt I did a great job interviewing the employees. I was able to check off every item on my list of things to look for at my next place of employment. I was also struck by how strongly the core values of CSAN came through in the words of the individual employees I spoke with. I liked this interview because they wanted to get to know about me as a person, not just what I could do for the company. The conversations wove back and forth between work and personal details. I could tell that many employees were friends both inside and outside the workplace. They genuinely cared about one another. I already felt valued, and I didn't even work here!

At the end of the interview I got a tour of the building. I noticed that numerous employee rewards were posted in various areas. There was a bulletin board titled "Catch Them Doing Something Good" with lots of pictures of employees at work. The whole atmosphere was positive. Once we were finished, Garrett invited me to join him and other employees for a social hour at a local restaurant. "We do this every Friday, Jack. Don't worry, this isn't part of the interview, so don't feel obligated to go. We just wanted to make sure we included you."

"Thanks," I said and decided to stop in for a half hour or so. That half hour turned into two hours, and Lisa actually ended up coming to join us for the last hour. I was glad I'd gone because I was able to talk with even more people and get to know them on a more personal level. It was a great day all around.

I'd walked into the interview wondering what we were going to do for five hours, and I was surprised at just how fast the time had gone. There was a lot of positive energy there. CSAN felt like a great opportunity for me, and it was definitely different from any company I'd ever considered before. I was not exactly sure how they felt about me, or whether they would be willing to overlook my lack of experience in some areas for this position. I was confident that I could do the job and do it well, but it still remained to be seen whether or not they believed that, too.

When Lisa and I arrived home, I told her all about the day. Her impression of the people she had met at the restaurant was very positive. I was glad that she'd had a chance to meet Garrett. In fact, Lisa had ended up speaking with him for a good half hour. Apparently, Garrett had been a counselor for children early in his career, so they had gotten along very well. Lisa was surprised that I had been able to tick off all the things on my list of what I was looking to find in an employer. "Sounds almost too good to be true," she said as she walked out of the family room and into the kitchen. She returned a few minutes later to tell me that I had a second interview with the drugstore company I'd interviewed with at the beginning of the week. They wanted me to meet late Monday afternoon. "That's very quick," I said to Lisa. "Rick said not to expect to hear anything for two weeks. This could be a good sign. Things are looking up."

Lisa and I discussed both opportunities in depth over the weekend, and I looked forward to my second interview. The day arrived quickly, and it went very well. What didn't go well, however, was the fact that I had to take another personal half day to go to this interview. My boss, Ian, was not pleased, to say the least.

I continued to feel very positive throughout the second interview. I was introduced to four more people, and, again, I was very comfortable. I asked lots of questions and was very thorough. There was something about having another job opportunity available that raised my confidence and made interviewing a breeze. Add the fact that I went into this process with a different perspective—*I* was interviewing *them*—and I was better able to pull out the information I wanted.

I was pleased that I could potentially have two solid job opportunities to choose from very soon. I spent the remainder of the week focused on my current job and getting caught up. Finally, on the following Wednesday, the big news arrived.

I was offered *both* jobs! Two companies extended me a formal offer of employment. Now I had a big decision to make, and I felt really torn. They were two great companies. I let both of them know that I needed the weekend to think things over and that I would call them first thing Monday morning.

FOURTEEN

Giving Back

Two years have gone by since that day, and I am proud to say that I am one of the two head coaches for Jake's soccer team. Jake is now in eighth grade, and it's hard to imagine that he's going to be in high school next year. Beckie's in sixth grade, and middle school is going very well for her. In addition to dance, she's taking piano lessons and playing basketball. I assist with the coaching of her team, too.

The past two years have been amazing. Life is so much more relaxed and so much more balanced. I don't carry around so much guilt anymore because I am diligent about fitting everything in and meeting all expectations—for myself, for my family, and for my work family, as I now refer to them. I also don't carry as much weight around anymore. I finally lost the twenty-five pounds I wanted to—and then some. I'm in better shape now than I was in college, and I feel great. My mind no longer races, and my stress level is low most of the time. I have a better relationship with each of my children, and my relationship with Lisa couldn't be better. We joke around often and remind one another about our BIG ROCKS. I've found that using the BIG ROCKS metaphor has been the icebreaker for us to talk about the things that matter most in our lives, which are one another, our family, and our careers.

In a sense, identifying our BIG ROCKS gave us the nudge we needed to get back to the fundamentals of our relationship and the importance of building quality relationships with others. Back in the days of Monaca, we didn't need to use metaphors like BIG ROCKS because it just sort of happened. But today we live in a different world. It's so much more chaotic, so busy and rushed. Each of us is guilty at some point in our lives of not slowing down enough to enjoy the things most important to us. Lisa and I still use the BIG ROCKS tools, too, especially our calendars. We use them to synchronize our schedules and to be respectful about letting each other know what we are doing. It eliminates any hard feelings or confusion. It has become a communication tool—our very own team-based approach to making our marriage and family work. We are both so grateful for learning about BIG ROCKS. This simple strategy forced us to identify what was important and then gave us simple tools to live it.

In the midst of my thoughts, I am waiting for the arrival of all of Jake's soccer team, my friend Tom Baker, who runs the team with me, and our assistant coach, Roy, who is notoriously twenty minutes late for most games. He doesn't work for CSAN, so I know how tough it is for him to get out on time for the games.

Tom and I have been working together at CSAN for the past two years. I ultimately chose to accept the position to head up their new division, and it's been one of the best decisions I've ever made. All of my expectations have been met, and I am doing a great job growing the division. When I started, there was only one other woman and me focusing on the new division. Now there are seven of us, and we've increased revenue by more than 200 percent over one year. Everyone is so helpful and team oriented that it drives me to do even better. I have a sense of ownership in my job and the company, and I won't fail either of them.

Using all of the principles Garrett has woven together based on numerous researched sources, we truly have a winning team and a winning corporate lifestyle. I feel very secure in my job and relaxed about knowing that I plan to be there long term. I love the people I work with, and I love what I do. Don't get me wrong; there are stressful days, and we have our challenges between team members, but at the end of the day we are a family. I also love the way the company operates. I find that because I have control over my own schedule, I work harder than before. I have a small office at home, and oftentimes I'll do a little work late at night after the kids have gone to bed. The trade-off is that I get to coach my son's and daughter's teams. I get to be involved in their lives, and I am a more productive and loyal employee as a result. The dynamics between all of us at work remind me of growing up in Monaca. There is always lots of noise, lots of play, lots of food in the office, and most of the time lots of fun. We work hard, but we play harder. All of us do things together outside work on occasion, and because of this I've not only found a great place to work but I've also made some great friends.

Tom walks in, bringing with him most of our team. Everyone suits up, and when all are present (except for our assistant coach, Roy, of course), we have our pregame pep talk and head out onto the field. The game begins, and Tom and I get to work. Right on schedule, Roy comes zipping into the parking lot and running across the field.

"I'm so sorry for being late," he tells us. "I just couldn't get out of the office, and I had to meet my wife for a doctor's appointment. We found out the sex of our baby today. We're having a boy!" he exclaims. "Man, I just don't know how I'm going to balance all of this. I have my wife, a baby on the way, a demanding career. ..." Roy stops speaking as he notices Tom and me looking at one another with really big smiles on our faces. "Why are you guys laughing ... what's the joke?"

Tom and I say in unison, "BIG ROCKS!"

"What are you guys talking about?" asks Roy.

"I'll tell you what, Roy, you keep your head in this game for the next forty minutes and then Tom and I are going to take you out for a pizza."

"Pizza? I don't have time to go out for a pizza. I need to get home."

"Roy, make time for Tom and me and a pizza. We want to tell you about BIG ROCKS. We used to be just like you until we found the secret to balancing our lives. Let me fill you in on BIG ROCKS ... it's your turn."

AFTERWORD

The story of BIG ROCKS was written as a parable. Jack, Lisa, and their children represent one type of typical family in the world today. Jack and Lisa are among those who grew up believing that if they followed a certain path and did everything "right," their lives would turn into the dream they had imagined for themselves. Like Jack and Lisa, we have all found that it is not as easy as we thought it would be when we were busy dreaming the dream.

Finding balance is hard work that requires continuous effort. We believe that it is possible for Jack, Lisa, and their family to achieve balance. We believe that there are good places to work out there. We mean in no way to minimize the fact that those opportunities of a "good place to work" are not plentiful in the world. And, when you are lucky enough to find that "good place to work," or to be part of creating it, balance can be achieved and alignment is possible for you as an individual—for you and your loved ones and for you and the bigger world that you fit into. If you are one of the lucky ones and believe that you have found that "good place to work," we would love it if you shared your experience with us by visiting our website at www.focuslifestyle.org.

As the husband and father to my personal family and as CEO and president of my own corporation, I believe I have a duty and an obligation to create this environment. I have found through experience that it is the most successful way to deliver personal and professional growth opportunities to all of the talented people I have chosen to surround myself with. I challenge each one of you who reads this book to do the same ... and when you achieve success, pass the message on.

NOTES

These notes contain information regarding the research studies supporting the opinions contained in this book. We have included these notes so that you, the reader, may seek further details pertaining to any specific areas of interest.

Chapter 2: Back to Reality
1. page 15   *"When was the last time you were offered any help—or better yet, skills training?"*
   The American Society of Trainers and Developers (ASTD) did a study of corporate training budgets titled *The 1998 ASTD State of the Industry Report,* January 1998. The report stated: "The growth in market-to-book ratios ... was more than twice as large for companies in the top half in 1996 training expenditures per employee [than] for companies in the bottom half." www.earlecompany.com/piedpiper2.htm

Chapter 3: Advice from the Sidelines
1. page 19   *People and their accomplishments weren't celebrated.*
   "A recent study found that work groups with positive interaction ratios greater than 3 to 1 are significantly more productive than teams that do not reach this ratio." Tom Rath and Dr. Donald O. Clifton, *How Full Is Your Bucket?* (New York: Gallup Press, 2004), p. 57.
2. page 19   *It frightened me that more than half the marriages in this country end in divorce. A simple coin toss could determine whether your marriage would succeed or fail.*
   John Gottman's pioneering research on marriages suggests there is a "magic ratio" of 5 to 1 in terms of our balance of positive to negative

interactions. "The fastest growing marital status category was divorced persons. The number [of] currently divorced adults quadrupled from 4.3 million in 1970 to 17.4 million in 1994." As cited by Arlene Saluter, *Marital Status and Living Arrangements: March 1994* (U.S. Bureau of the Census, March 1996), series P20-484, p. vi.

CHAPTER 5: TAKING INITIATIVE: LEARNING ABOUT BIG ROCKS

1. page 30   *"I like to come to this series of seminars because so far at each one, I have taken away at least one thing that inspired me to make a positive change in my life."*

The Focus LifeStyle™ is the property of The Focus Group Limited. The Focus LifeStyle is a style of living, a way of life. Individuals have lifestyles, and so do organizations. Lifestyles are chosen; cultures are imposed.

The Focus LifeStyle is a people process for the people age. In basic terms, it aligns people's thoughts, feelings, and actions, activating human potential and maximizing performance, thus creating engagement.

The Focus LifeStyle will lift people beyond their own vision of capability. The underlying processes that create the Focus LifeStyle enable messages to be more effectively delivered and received, strengthening communication and interaction at work, home, or play.

For more information, see the "Services Available" section at the end of this book.

CHAPTER 6: BELIEVING: THE BIG ROCKS PHILOSOPHY

1. page 42   *"Alignment happens when individuals are able to get their thoughts, feelings, and actions consistent within themselves and with those around them."*

Dr. Gary F. Russell, "An Explanation of the Human Behavioral System," data collection/interpretation 1994–2004.

2. page 42   *"I learned that by meeting the needs of the people within my organization, business success surely followed."*

"AC Nielsen ... states that it finds that when employee satisfaction rises, financial results soon improve." Sue Shellenbarger, "Surveys Link Satisfaction of Employees, Customers," *Wall Street Journal,* January 25, 1999.

3. page 46   *"How many of you have been praised for a job well done over the past two weeks?"*

"65% of Americans received no recognition in the workplace last year." Tom Rath and Dr. Donald O. Clifton, *How Full Is Your Bucket?* (New York: Gallup Press, 2004), p. 40.

4. page 47   *"To provide perspective, in the United States, 74 percent of our workforce admits to not being engaged or being actively disengaged."*

"The continued tracking of engagement by Gallup is very encouraging. It shows that many not-engaged employees can be considered 'in transit.' They are waiting for an opportunity to become fully engaged." Curt Coffman and Gabriel Gonzalez-Molina, *Follow this Path* (New York: Warner Books, 2002), p. 131.

"Highly dedicated employees are found across the age spectrum. In GMJ's fourth national survey of U.S. workers, the percentage who say they are engaged, or deeply involved in their work, varied only slightly by age group: 35% of workers ages 18 to 24 are engaged; as are 29% ages 25 to 34; 30% ages 35 to 49; and 29% ages 50 and older." Teresa Tritch, "Talk of Ages," *Gallup Management Journal*, December 15, 2001, http://gmj.gallup.com/

The longer employees stay with their company the less engaged they become

First 6 Months   6 Months to 3 Years   After 10 Years

50% 12% 38%   55% 18% 27%   57% 23% 20%

■ Engaged   ■ Not Engaged   Actively Not Engaged

SOURCE: GALLUP ORGANIZATION

- First six months: 38 percent engaged, 50 percent not engaged, 12 percent actively disengaged
- Six months–three years: 27 percent engaged, 55 percent not engaged, 18 percent actively disengaged
- Three years–ten years: 22 percent engaged, 66 percent not engaged, 22 percent actively disengaged

- After ten years: 20 percent engaged, 67 percent not engaged, 23 percent actively disengaged

Coffman and Gonzalez-Molina, *Follow this Path*, p. 136.

5. page 47   *"Lead indicators provide an understanding of whether or not the group of people working in any organization is poised and willing to drive the company in the direction that meets both the company's vision and its financial projections."*

"Paying attention to these many local human interactions helps businesses of every stripe meet that one big objective—higher revenues and earnings—more surely than focusing on financials alone. Gallup has even coined a term for the process of achieving this most desirable blend: optimization." William J. McEwen, "The Power of the Fifth P.," *Gallup Management Journal*, March 15, 2001, http://gmj.gallup.com/

"Lag indicators, that is they measure past performance, whilst the process and learning and growth perspectives measure investments in activities which create future value, and are therefore lead indicators." Taken from The Balanced Scorecard. The Balanced Scorecard, a new approach to strategic management, was developed by Robert Kaplan and David Norton, from the Harvard Business School, in the early 1990s. http://www.balancedscorecard.org

6. page 49   *"This is key because the average rate of retention for businesses around the globe today is 3.4 years."*

"The average employee stays in his job 3.4 years." Marc Drizin, "Employees: Recruitment, Retention, and Loyalty," February 28, 2002. www.crmguru.com

"A recent study of employee-turnover expenses at 206 medium to large companies by William M. Mercer, Inc., an economic analysis firm, found that replacing a worker cost on average between $10,000 and $30,000 and often even more." Patricia P. Pine, Ph.D., "Older Workers: Retirement or Continued Work?" *The Future of Aging in New York State* (2000). http://aging.state.ny.us/explore/project2015/artolderworkers.htm

7. page 49   *"In fact, Richard Sennett, a sociologist at New York University has calculated that a young American today with at least two years of college can expect to change jobs eleven times before retirement."*

John Schwartz, "Workplace Stress: Americans' Bugaboo," *New York Times*, Sunday, September 5, 2004, p. D2.

CHAPTER 7: BIG ROCKS TOOL BOX 1: BIG ROCKS IDENTIFICATION

1. page 53   *"For years, American businesses have pointed to Japanese workers as a model of productivity and teamwork. The Japanese prided themselves on Total Quality Management (TQM)."*

TQM is "a system of continuous improvement employing participative management and centered on the needs of customers." "Key components of TQM are employee involvement and training, problem-solving teams, statistical methods, long-term goals and thinking, and recognition that the system, not people, produces inefficiencies." S. Jurow and S. B. Barnard, "Introduction: TQM Fundamentals and Overview of Contents," *Journal of Library Administration,* 18(1/2) (1993): 1–13 (EJ 469 099).

2. page 58   *"Too many corporations and businesses hold strongly to the belief that maximizing the number of hours an employee works results in maximized productivity. It simply isn't true. Maximizing hours eventually leads to diminished productivity, employee resentment, and diminished retention."*

"A Watson Wyatt Worldwide study found that the practice of maintaining a collegial, flexible workplace is associated with the second-largest increase in shareholder value (9 percent), suggesting that employee satisfaction is directly related to financial gain." Bruce Pfau and Ira Kay, "The Hidden Human Resource: Shareholder Value—Finding the Right Blend of Rewards, Flexibility, and Technology to Manage Your People Adds Measurable Value to the Corporate Bottom Line." *Optimize,* no. 8 (June 2002). http://www.optimizemagazine.com/issue/008/culture.htm

CHAPTER 9: BIG ROCKS TOOL BOX 3: LIFESTYLE LIFELINES

1. page 72   *"Individual contribution leads to ownership, and hopefully we all recognize that if you are part of creating something, or have ownership in it, then you are more effective in implementing it."*

"Employee productivity depends on the amount of time an individual is physically present at a job and also the degree to which he or she is 'mentally present' or efficiently functioning while present at a job." Ron Goetzel and Ronald Ozminkowski, "Health Productivity Management Assists Benefits Business Strategy," *Employee Benefit News* (October 15, 1999). http://www.integratedbenefitsinstitute.org/news/articles/1999/10/

2. page 74   *"Did you ever stop to analyze how much time was spent on what you were doing well versus how much time was spent on the areas in which*

you needed improvement? If you did analyze it, you might find that the majority of the time was spent on your weaknesses."

"They become expert in those areas where their employees struggle, delicately rename these 'skill gaps' or 'areas of opportunity,' and then pack them off to training classes so that the weaknesses can be fixed.

"But this isn't development, it is damage control. And by itself damage control is a poor strategy for elevating either the employee or the organization to world-class performance." *Gallup Management Journal,* "The Strengths Revolution." Excerpted from Marcus Buckingham and Donald O. Clifton, *Now, Discover Your Strengths* (New York: Free Press, 2001).

"Most of us have grown up in a culture in which it's much easier to tell people what they did wrong than to praise them when they succeed. Although this negativity-based approach might have evolved unintentionally, it nevertheless permeates our society at all levels." Tom Rath and Dr. Donald O. Clifton, *How Full Is Your Bucket?* (New York: Gallup Press, 2004), p. 47.

3. page 75   *"Having a best friend at work or cultivating great friendships in the work environment elevates a person's level of engagement, which ultimately leads to increased productivity and corporate profit."*

"Having a best friend at work improves a person's chances of being engaged by an amazing 54 percent. Not having one, on the other hand, reduces it to zero." Curt Coffman and Gabriel Gonzalez-Molina, *Follow this Path* (New York: Warner Books, 2002), p. 90.

4. page 81   *"So, when I identified the correlation between meeting my employees' needs and the success of my business, I wanted to capture those intangible steps. I now refer to the intangible steps that work to enable and engage employees as 'people processes.'"*

Dr. Gary F. Russell, "An Explanation of the Human Behavioral System," data collection/interpretation 1994–2004.

5. page 82   Russell, data collection/interpretation, 1994–2004.

6. page 83   *"Absenteeism … is a billion-dollar problem every year in this country. Across the world it is a trillion-dollar problem."*

"When you add workplace injury, illness, turnover, absences, and fraud, the cost could surpass $1 trillion per year, or nearly 10% of the U.S. gross domestic product (GDP). These costs are not specific to the United States; they exist to varying degrees in every country, industry, and organization we have studied." Rath and Clifton, *How Full Is Your Bucket?* p. 33.

7. page 83   *"One of the greatest contributors to my own business success is that I'm a firm believer in the notion that people need to plan their vacation time, and they need to take it."*

"Many European nations have national laws requiring that everyone who has been working at least a year get a decent vacation. In France and Denmark, it's five weeks minimum. In Spain, it's 30 days, in Norway four weeks and a day, and in the Netherlands four weeks." Thane Peterson, "Take a Break, and the Rest Is Easy," *Business Week Online*, August 28, 2001. http://www.businessweek.com/bwdaily/dnflash/aug2001/nf20010828_6 16.htm

"It's well documented that Americans work more and play less than citizens of any other industrialized nation. [In the U.S. there is no requirement that any form of paid vacation time be granted to private-sector employees.] The 14 days of paid vacation and holidays received on average by U.S. workers are but half of what their counterparts receive in many European countries where employers generally must provide at least four weeks of paid leave annually." Bill Rotstein, "Who Needs a Vacation? Not These Happy Workers," August 24, 2003. www.post-gazette.com

CHAPTER 10: BIG ROCKS TOOL BOX 4: ACTIVELY LIVING BIG ROCKS

1. page 97   *"I changed jobs because of long hours and feeling underappreciated."*

"The survey found that fewer than one in five respondents perceive themselves to be in roles that give them opportunities to do what they do best every day. One in three respondents consider themselves to be miscast in their current roles."

Ashok Gopal, "Disengaged Employees Cost Singapore $4.9 Billion," *Gallup Management Journal*, October 9, 2003. Gmj.gallup.com/content/default.asp?ca=1207

"The #1 reason people leave their jobs: They don't feel appreciated." Tom Rath and Dr. Donald O. Clifton, *How Full Is Your Bucket?* (New York: Gallup Press, 2004), p. 31.

CHAPTER 11: COURAGE TO CHANGE

1. page 102   *"Personally speaking, I'd always been more motivated by receiving time off to spend with my family."*

Some workers would take a pay cut or forgo a raise in exchange for more vacation time:

Less than $35,000: 19%

$35,001 to $49,999: 12%

$50,000 to $74,999: 11%

$75,000 or more: 25%

"Some Workers Willing to Pay for More Vacation Time," (Final Edition), *USA Today*, July 15, 2004, p. B01. Expedia's Vacation Deprivation survey of 2,019 respondents conducted in May. Margin of error = –4 percentage points.

Focus

LifeStyle

SERVICES AVAILABLE

WHAT IS DIFFERENT ABOUT THE FOCUS GROUP?

Sometimes it takes trying something really different, something truly unique, to get the outcomes you're looking for. The Focus Group is different, but then again so are the times we live in, and so is the world. Are you thinking differently than you used to? Is your organization? What are your chances for survival? Different circumstances call for different measures—a new way of thinking, a new way of conducting our daily lives and affairs. After over thirty years of behavioral research and practical application with a myriad of businesses, the Focus Group is now giving you the key to survival. The **Focus LifeStyle** is a **People Process for the People Age™,** and a process, although it cannot be seen, that is as vital to sustaining an organization as oxygen is to sustaining life.

HOW EXACTLY DOES THE FOCUS GROUP CREATE A FOCUS LIFESTYLE WITHIN A COMPANY?

The Focus Group understands that having an external provider or consultant is no longer viable for any organization. It's obsolete. That's why we are an internal provider. We become part of your organization and are there for you year-round. We don't work with hundreds of clients each year; we select just five or six, allowing us to become a partner in the systems and processes that you need to effectively maximize your employees' individual and collective talents. This program doesn't just develop employees who are happier and more productive—it extends to every facet of your organization, all the way to your external clients and consumers.

As part of this new and different world of business, we all know that the role of management has shifted to becoming a "leader of people." *Leadership* is the key to people development, whereas having managers who control systems and physical processes is simply a given. But, just as the argument that technology was going to replace paper is now hollow unless there are proven processes that can demonstrate and provide substance to the statement, so, too, when arguing over the move from managers to leaders, we must provide concrete methods and processes that have been researched and proven to be effective. Asking people to become leaders is a nice concept, but that's all it is unless we can provide a new way of creating better interactions between people.

This is where the Focus Group steps in because we have a new and different people program call the **Focus LifeStyle**. We have two researched and tested systems within the **Focus LifeStyle** that provide two basic, but necessary, processes for organizations of the future. The first system is Alignment, which lines up the thoughts, feelings, and actions between two to thousands of people. In an organization, this is called "client alignment." An organization's greatest challenge is to take an idea or product and deliver it consistently to one or thousands of people. Alignment makes this issue go away. The second system, Activation, has a process for interaction. People have always had the energy for change and greatness within them, yet they are typically expected to effect change or perform from outside stimulus, called "motivation." Once activated, the "giant within" is awakened and the employee becomes engaged, which helps with retention of staff. Face it, if your staff isn't engaged (activated to stay), what makes you think your consumers are?

It's a different world we live in—the consumer is in charge, and your staff should now be viewed as part of that group. Don't you think you need something different to deal with these challenges you are facing? These are difficult times. The **Focus LifeStyle** not only develops employees of character but also, more importantly, provides you with an internal partner who works with you. The Focus Group supplies you with all the tools you need to develop the staff and organization you always dreamed of, and together we will help you reach your goals.

CONTACT INFORMATION

The Focus Group Limited
47 Water Street, Suite 101
Mystic, CT 06355
1-860-572-8882 (phone)
1-860-536-3308 (fax)
www.focuslifestyle.org